DESTINATION NE250

The North East 250 Road Trip
Scotland's Best Kept Secret - Harbours, Castles, and Endless Beaches

Gemma Kerr and Campbell Kerr
Destination Earth Guides

99 Lairig Ghru

FOREWORD

No matter how far we've travelled, how many countries we've explored, or how many miles we've clocked up on planes, trains and campervans, nowhere ever quite captures our hearts like Scotland does. There's a wildness to it. A magic. A sense of coming home, whether you're from here or just passing through.

When we bought Ellie, our trusty (or if you follow us on socials, not so trusty!) motorhome, we had no idea just how much of an adventure she'd take us on. When we were ready to hit the road there was one place we knew had to be our very first road trip. A journey along a coastline we'd long overlooked. A stretch of Scotland that, even today, remains one of its best kept secrets and as we trundled through its colourful fishing villages, stood amongst the castle ruins with the wind in our hair, and parked up by golden beaches that could rival anywhere in the world, we knew we'd found something truly special.

After this first trip, we soon found ourselves returning to this part of Scotland more and more, spending all seasons exploring new spots in every weather imaginable. We turned over every rock (sometimes literally), followed every winding track, and spoke to as many locals as we could, all to make sure we experienced as much of it as possible. The deeper we explored, the more we realised that this was one of Scotland's most special places. A true hidden gem of a road trip.

We also realised that this book would not be complete without a special mention of one of our favourite places in Scotland. For both Gemma and I, the Cairngorms National Park holds a special place in our hearts. It's where we spent many childhood holidays, running wild amongst the ancient forests, swimming in the lochs, and being awed by those towering mountains. Even now, it's a place that feels like home every time we visit. That's why we've expanded this guide to include the heart of the Highlands, giving you the chance to explore the wild places that mean so much to us.

This book is the result of countless miles on the road, sleepless nights in the van, and more cups of coffee than we care to admit. It's a labour of love, and one we've poured our hearts into. Whether you're here for the history, the beaches, the hikes, or the whisky, we hope this guide helps you plan the most unforgettable road trip of your life through one of Scotland's best kept secrets.

And who knows, you might just fall in love with it like we did.

ABOUT THE AUTHORS

We are Gemma and Campbell, a Scottish couple with a passion for travel and adventure. Before the release of our first book, we were creating online content in the form of written travel guides and ebooks that aspiring travellers could use to plan their trips.

Following on from the unexpected and incredible success of our other Destination Earth Guide books, which we are eternally grateful for the support and enthusiasm our community has shown, we have decided to write about another one of our favourite places in Scotland, the North East 250 road trip.

Over the past year, we have explored Scotland in great depth in our motorhome, finding the best places for you to add to your adventure list and make the most of your trip to Scotland. The memories that have been created whilst exploring these places are unforgettable and we hope that you can enjoy an adventure on the North East 250 as much as we do.

Vanlife Adventures
Instagram - @highlands2hammocks
Youtube - Highlands2hammocks

Travel Guides & Inspiration
Instagram - @Destinationearth.guides
Youtube - Destination Earth Guides

Acknowledgements

We would like to dedicate this book to our families, with their never-ending support of our decision to set off on this alternative life, and to our friends who have stood beside us, forever understanding of the hours of work that this lifestyle requires and always being there for us when we come home to rest.

Surround yourself with those who love you, support you, and inspire you, and there is nothing you cannot do.

A special thank you must also be extended to our colleagues and friends Shiva Shahriari and Natasha Gooch for their help in putting this book together and the vast amount of research that has been involved.

CONTENTS

Summary of Route 2
Introduction 3
What to Expect 19
The Rugged Side of the NE250 27
Best of the North East 250 46

BRAEMAR & ROYAL DEESIDE 67
ABERDEEN 87
THE EAST COAST 105
MORAY & THE SUNSHINE COAST 122
DUFFTOWN & THE WHISKY TRAIL 149
THE CAIRNGORMS 167

Planning Your Trip
- Five Day Itinerary 191
- Ten Day Itinerary 194
- Fourteen Day Itinerary 199

82 Leith Hall Garden & Estate

Summary of the North East 250

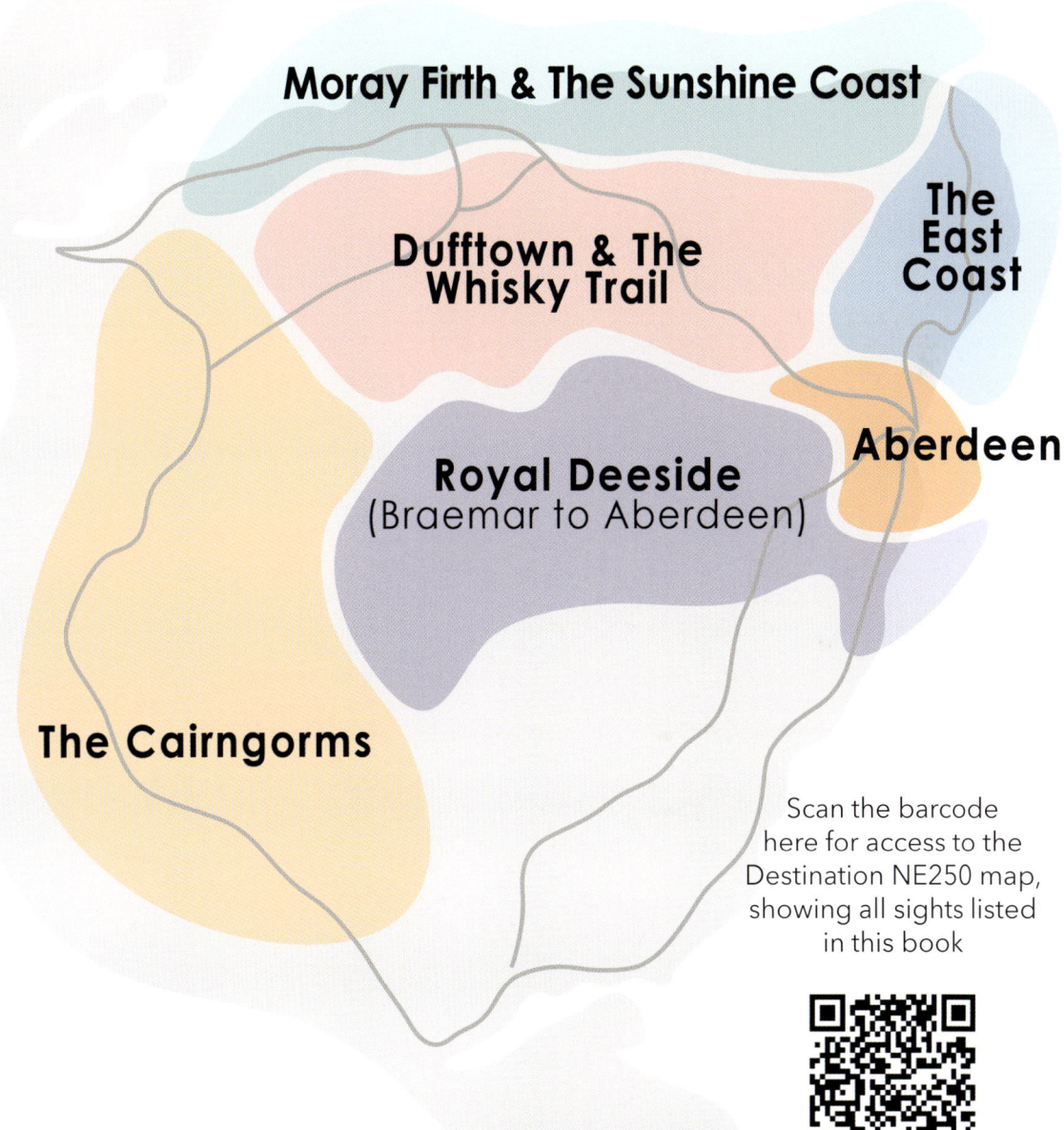

Scan the barcode here for access to the Destination NE250 map, showing all sights listed in this book

Introduction

A part of Scotland full of ancient history, rich traditions, and a unique language, Scotland's North East 250 is one of the country's most fascinating and diverse road trips. From the rugged peaks of the Cairngorms to the dramatic cliffs of the Moray Firth, from grand castles and whisky distilleries to charming fishing villages and bustling cities, the NE250 offers a slice of Scotland that's often overlooked. Yet it is an unforgettable adventure for those who make the journey.

This region has its own rhythm and way of life, shaped by centuries of seafaring, farming, and whisky making. It's a place where the Doric language still rings out in everyday conversation, where folklore and legend live on, and where communities are fiercely proud of their heritage. The landscapes are as varied as the stories with wild mountains, ancient pine forests, windswept beaches, and rolling farmland, all within easy reach of one another. One moment you're exploring the ruins of a medieval castle perched on a cliff edge, the next you're sampling a dram at one of the world's most famous distilleries.

The NE250 is made for those who want to dive deeper into Scotland's culture and history, and experience a side of the country that's both authentic and awe-inspiring. Whether you're drawn by the thought of spotting dolphins leaping in the Moray Firth, hiking remote trails in the Cairngorms, or wandering the cobbled streets of fishing towns like Pennan and Cullen, this route has something for everyone.

In this book, we'll share our extensive knowledge and first hand experience of the NE250, after months of exploring its every corner. We've braved the four seasons in a single day, met locals who made us feel like family, and uncovered hidden gems you won't find on every tourist map. You'll find everything you need here to plan your perfect trip, whether you're travelling by motorhome, car, or bike, including where to eat, stay, and explore along the way.

We hope this guide inspires you to discover why we believe the NE250 is one of Scotland's best road trips, and that your own adventure here is every bit as unforgettable as ours was. Get ready to fall in love with the heart and soul of the North East.

47 Crovie Village Viewpoint

What is the NE250?

The North East 250 road trip encompasses the region known as the shoulder of Scotland, spanning north from Aberdeen around the Moary coastal region. It covers an area of just over 3300 sqaure miles and contains everything from the dramatic mountains of the Cairngorms to the beautiful stretches of sand along the Moray coast, such as Rattray Head Beach.

Unlike the more isolated Highlands, the NE250 offers a perfect blend of wild beauty and welcoming towns, easily accessed from major hubs like Aberdeen. Whether you begin your journey in the city, at the edge of the Cairngorms, or along the Moray Firth coast, you will find excellent roads, charming villages, and countless opportunities for adventure, all without the long empty stretches you find elsewhere in Scotland.

The region you will explore along the NE250 is full of history. This land was once the stronghold of powerful Scottish clans, a centre of medieval politics, and a playground for royalty like Queen Victoria herself. The castles of Aberdeenshire, including fairytale Craigievar, dramatic Dunnottar, and the royal residence at Balmoral, are among the finest in the world, each telling stories of war, romance, and rebellion. Along the coast, the fishing communities of Pennan, Cullen, and Footdee still echo with tales of the sea, while inland, whisky distilleries and farm shops invite you to taste centuries of local tradition.

Of course, the weather plays its own part in the adventure around the NE250. The North Sea storms roll in fast, the mist clings to the hills and fields, and sunshine can break through the clouds in the blink of an eye. This ever changing climate is what keeps the landscape lush and alive, from the heather strewn mountains of the Cairngorms to the wind swept beaches of the Moray Coast.

You can expect to find incredible landmarks scattered throughout your journey such as the white sands of Newburgh Beach (where you might spot a seal colony), the mighty cliffs beneath Slains Castle (rumoured to have inspired Bram Stoker's Dracula), and the ancient standing stones that dot the countryside like relics of a forgotten world. You will also drive over the Cairnwell Pass, the highest main road in the UK, offering breathtaking views across the rugged peaks and glens of the eastern Highlands. From the quiet peace of Speyside's whisky trails to the crashing surf of the Banffshire coast, the NE250 is bursting with variety and different interests for everyone.
Despite its rich, remote beauty, the North East 250 is remarkably accessible. Thanks to

Aberdeen's airport, rail links, and excellent roads, it is easy to reach and just as easy to lose yourself in. In fact, its accessibility and compactness make it perfect for those wanting a taste of Scotland's wilderness, history, and culture, without needing to venture too far from modern comforts or transport.

No matter when you visit, the North East 250 promises a road trip that is more than just scenic. It is an unforgettable experience of heritage, landscape, flavour, and story. Every turn in the road reveals something different, a hidden waterfall, a cosy café, a breathtaking castle ruin, or a deserted golden beach. Adventure, peace, history, and beauty, the NE250 is Scotland, distilled into one epic loop.

38 Rattray Head Lighthouse

How to Get Around the NE250

Deciding how to tour the North East 250 is entirely up to you. If you prefer the freedom of the open road in a campervan there are many great campsites and aries around the route or if you prefer the comfort of a car with cosy overnight stays, there are also a large amount of accommodation options on the NE250.

Drive it by Car
One of the most popular ways to experience the NE250 is by car. The full circular route spans around 250 miles, making it manageable over a long weekend or a more relaxed week or two week-long escape. There are plenty of hotels, B&Bs, guesthouses and unique accommodations along the way which we will detail more of in each section.

Tour in a Campervan
For the ultimate freedom, touring the NE250 by campervan is a fantastic option. There are many beautiful campsites where you can wake up to seafront views or be surrounded by the mountains. It also allows you more flexibility on the road to travel at your own pace.

If you don't own a campervan and are travelling up to the NE250 through Glasgow, we would love to introduce you to our vans for hire at Scotland Escape. Based at Glasgow airport, we offer high quality vans ready for adventure, as well as tailored trip planning services for the perfct road trip experience, and as a reader of this book please get in touch with us for a special discount www.scotlandescape.com

Fly In and Hire
If you are travelling from further afield you might want to fly into Aberdeen International Airport, or Inverness Airport just a short drive from the route. Here you will have the option to pick up a hire car or campervan and start your trip from there. If you are tight on time, this may be the fastest way to explore the region.

Cycle Routes
If you are feeling active, parts of the NE250 can be explored by bike. The coastal sections are especially well-suited to cycling, with relatively flat terrain and spectacular sea views. Some of the inland stretches are more challenging, with steep hills and winding roads, so good planning (and strong legs!) are essential.

Public Transport
Whilst having your own vehicle makes the route a lot easier to explore fully, sections of the NE250 are accessible by public transport. Buses link many of the main towns and villages, and there are train stations in Aberdeen, Keith, and Huntly. Public transport isn't frequent in rural areas, so this option works best for those with time and flexibility.

Extend Your Adventure by Ferry
If your appetite for exploring Scotland continues beyond the NE250, Aberdeen Ferry Terminal provides regular sailings to Orkney and Shetland operated by NorthLink Ferries. These overnight crossings are an excellent way to extend your road trip into the Northern Isles, where you can explore dramatic coastlines, Viking history, and the unique island culture. Both foot passengers and vehicles are welcome on board.

History of the NE250

With a history stretching back thousands of years, the North East 250 route tells the story of Scotland's ancient past, woven through every village, castle ruin and coastal view. This corner of Scotland has been home to Neolithic settlers, the enigmatic Picts, Norse invaders, powerful Highland clans and Victorian royalty. Today, many of those historical sights still lie there as we follow in their footsteps, discovering stone circles, Pictish symbol stones, medieval strongholds and grand baronial estates around our NE250 road trip.

The terrain in this part of Scotland is some of the oldest in the UK, forged over hundreds of millions of years by ancient volcanic activity, shifting tectonic plates, and glacial erosion. To the south, the Cairngorm Mountains are what remains of an immense, ancient mountain range and to the north, the Moray Firth coastline showcases fossil-rich rock formations, with its cliffs and caves sculpted over millennia by relentless wind and sea.
Throughout the centuries, this region has been the stronghold of powerful Scottish clans, including the Gordons, Frasers, and Forbes. They left behind a legacy of castles, from the

ruined Auchindoun and Balvenie to the currently occupied fortress of Braemar Castle. Speyside has also evolved into the heart of Scotland's whisky industry, with world famous distilleries lining the River Spey, while bustling fishing ports like Cullen, Buckie and Banff tell tales of the boom and bust herring trade.

Royal Deeside found fame in the Victorian era, when Queen Victoria fell in love with the area and made Balmoral Castle a royal retreat which is a tradition that is continued by the Royal Family to this day. Meanwhile, Aberdeen, also known as the "Granite City", grew into a global centre of the oil industry in the 20th century.

And running through it all is the Doric language, a traditional Scots dialect spoken across Aberdeenshire and Moray for generations. You might hear locals speaking it as you travel around the region.

The Unique Culture - Doric

Doric is a cultural cornerstone of north-east Scotland and you may hear many of the locals speak it on your travels around the NE250. Doric is a term that originates from Ancient Greece, used to differentiate the rural dialect from the urban dialect of Athens. It is rumoured to have been adopted by Scots due to the similarity in cultural divide between the Highlands and the Lowlands. For decades it has been argued whether Doric is a language or a dialect but one thing that is known, is that speaking in Doric will help keep it alive.

Historically, Doric was spoken across much of the old Grampian region and it has been passed down orally through generations. It was once the everyday language of crofters, fisherfolk, and traders, and though often overlooked in official settings, it has seen a revival in recent decades, with schools, broadcasters, and writers embracing it with renewed pride, determined to keep Doric alive.

17 Footdee

Doric is a Scots dialect traditionally spoken in the northeast of Scotland, particularly in Aberdeenshire, Moray, and parts of Angus. Here are some interesting facts about Doric:

Ancient Roots - Doric Scots evolved from the Germanic languages brought to Scotland by the Angles in the early medieval period and has been influenced by Old Norse due to Viking settlements.

Distinct Vocabulary - It has many unique words and phrases, such as fit like? (how are you?), loon (boy), quine (girl), and foos yer doos? (how's it going?).

Pronunciation Differences - Doric features distinct sounds, including a rolling 'r' and the tendency to soften or omit certain consonants, making it sound quite different from standard English or even other Scots dialects.

Literary and Cultural Significance - Many poets and writers, such as Charles Murray and Sheena Blackhall, have written in Doric, helping to preserve and promote the dialect.

Not Just Rural - While often associated with farming and fishing communities, Doric is still spoken in Aberdeen and other urban areas in the northeast.

Recognised as Part of Scots - Doric is a variety of the Scots language, which has official recognition as a regional language in Scotland. Efforts to preserve and promote Doric include education initiatives and Doric festivals.

Here are some common Doric phrases and their English translations:

Fit like? – How are you?
Nae bad, yersel'? – Not bad, yourself?
Foo's yer doos? – How's it going? (Literally, "How are your pigeons?")
Far aboots are ye fae? – Where are you from?
Gie's a bosie! – Give me a hug!
Aye, nae bother! – Yes, no problem!
Dinna fash yersel' – Don't worry about it.
Ye're aff yer heid! – You're crazy!
I'm fair scunnered – I'm really fed up.
Hav ye seen ma piece? – Have you seen my sandwich? (Piece means sandwich in Scots.)
He's a richt chancer. – He's a real opportunist.
Yon's a rare nicht. – That's a great night.
Away an bile yer heid! – Go away and stop talking nonsense!

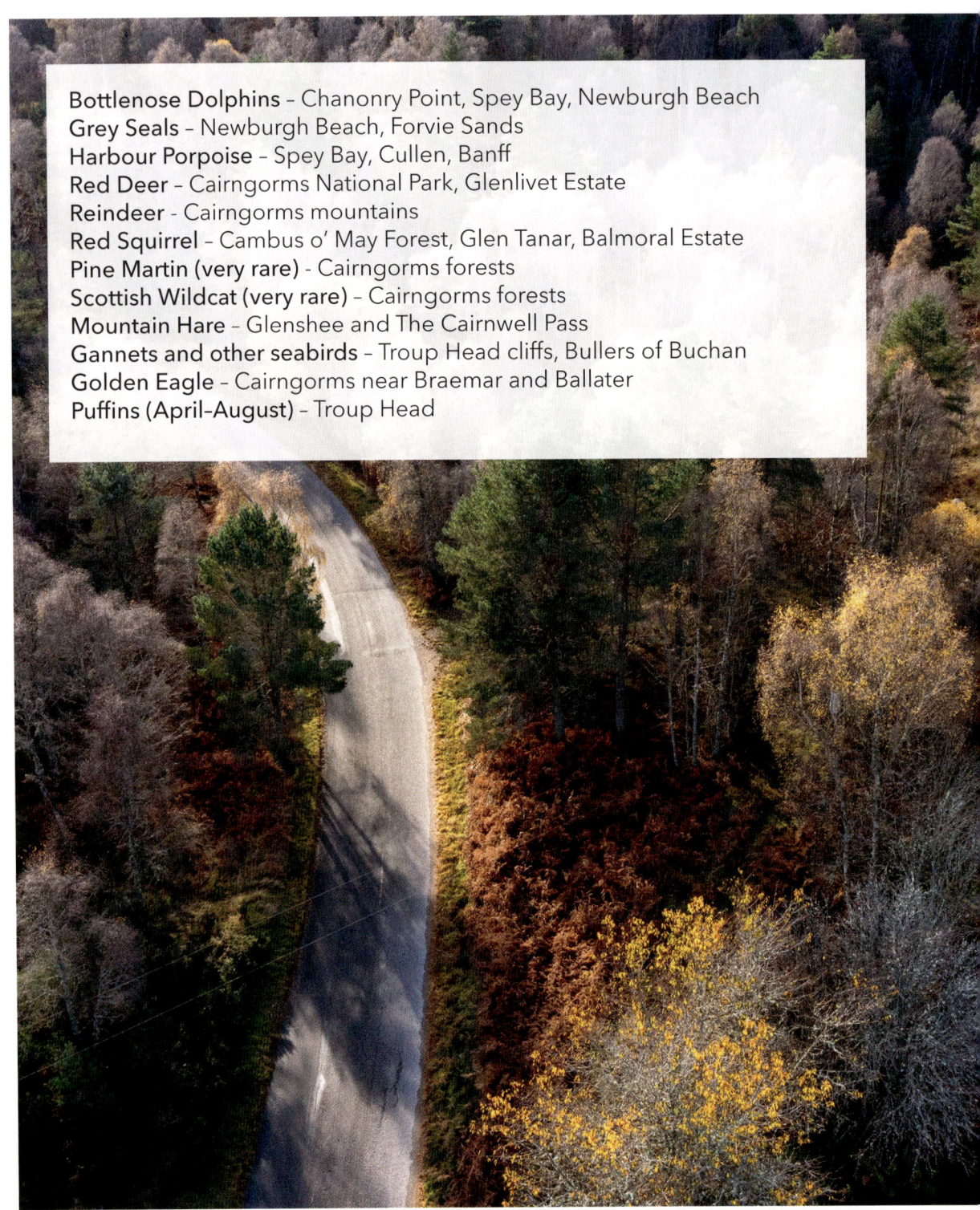

Bottlenose Dolphins – Chanonry Point, Spey Bay, Newburgh Beach
Grey Seals – Newburgh Beach, Forvie Sands
Harbour Porpoise – Spey Bay, Cullen, Banff
Red Deer – Cairngorms National Park, Glenlivet Estate
Reindeer - Cairngorms mountains
Red Squirrel – Cambus o' May Forest, Glen Tanar, Balmoral Estate
Pine Martin (very rare) - Cairngorms forests
Scottish Wildcat (very rare) – Cairngorms forests
Mountain Hare – Glenshee and The Cairnwell Pass
Gannets and other seabirds – Troup Head cliffs, Bullers of Buchan
Golden Eagle – Cairngorms near Braemar and Ballater
Puffins (April-August) – Troup Head

Wildlife on the NE250

The landscape of the NE250 as it stretches from the rugged Cairngorms National Park, across to Aberdeen, and sweeps around the Moray Coast to Findhorn, is a journey through some of Scotland's most diverse and fascinating scenery. As you travel east through the towering granite mountains, through the thick ancient forests before the landscape shifts into rolling farmland meeting windswept coastlines. All of which offer a perfect sanctuary for Scotland's wildlife to thrive.

Along the Moray Firth coastline look out for pods of bottlenose dolphins often dancing in the waves, while seals laze on quiet beaches like those at Newburgh. Whilst in the Cairngorms you will want to keep your eyes peeled for the red squirrels that flit through Caledonian pine forests and the red deer roam the hillsides, and if you're lucky If you are really lucky, you might even spot the elusive golden eagle soaring above.

The rivers and lochs around this region are rich with salmon and trout, and in spring, capercaillie and ospreys return to their Highland nesting grounds.

If you are on the look out for some hairy coos, you might be lucky enough to bump into a few along the route.

Popularity of the NE250

The North East 250 was officially launched in November 2017, envisioned by Guy Macpherson-Grant the owner of Ballindalloch Castle, to stimulate tourism and economic growth in Scotland's north-east and ever since the NE250 has been gaining popularity as a scenic (and much quieter) alternative to the North Coast 500.

In response to the surge in campervan tourism, Moray Council has initiated a consultation to manage overnight stays for campervans and motorhomes at designated council-owned locations. The proposed scheme aims to provide convenient short-stay parking options while addressing community concerns and promoting sustainable tourism. Provisional sites under consideration include Lossiemouth, Cullen, Buckie, Forres, Portgordon, Burghead, Ballindalloch, Craigellachie, and Aberlour.

Additionally, Forestry and Land Scotland has expanded its "**Stay the Night**" initiative, allowing self-contained motorhomes and campervans to park overnight at designated car parks across Scotland. Recent additions to this scheme include Donview in Aberdeenshire and the coastal forest at Culbin in Moray, further accommodating the needs of touring visitors .

These developments reflect a broader trend in Scotland, where the number of motorhome and campervan trips has been on the rise. In 2022 alone, domestic visitors made approximately 1.58 million such trips, contributing £355 million to the economy . The NE250, with its rich offerings and increasing infrastructure, continues to be a compelling choice for travellers seeking a unique Scottish experience.

This is all great news for all roadtrippers, both in a campervan as well as in a car, as it shows an increasing trend for investment into the hospitality and tourism industry in these beautiful and remote areas. It also allows campervan or motorhome owners looking to visit these vulnerable areas responsibly to do so more easily, proving that the road trip way of life is only just getting started.

Alternative Road Trips to the NE250

The North East 250 is Aberdeenshire's answer to the popular **NC500** road trip, combining coastal views and beaches, whisky trails, plenty of castles and a mountain wilderness all in one short and easily accessible loop.

Beyond the north eastern circuit of the **NE250**, there are plenty more adventures to discover. The **Heart 200** takes you through the central Highlands and Perthshire's historic heartland. To the west, the **Argyll Coastal Route** offers lochside drives and links to Scotland's incredible islands.

The **Fife Coastal Route** and the **Angus Coastal Trail** are perfect for a relaxed journey of fishing villages and hidden beaches, while the **South West 300** explores Dumfries and Galloway's rugged beauty and stunning coastline.

Whilst you are in the area, you may wish to extend your travels further and take the opportunity to take the overnight NorthLink ferry from Aberdeen to **Orkney** and **Shetland**, two of Scotland's most remote and fascinating archipelagos, each steeped in Viking history, rich wildlife, and magnificent scenery.

Following road trips are a great way to see the best of what a place has to offer so after your NE250 road trip, how about trying another one of Scotland's epic adventures?!

What to Expect from the NE250

Expect quieter roads than the NC500, a slower pace of life, and plenty of hidden gems without the tourist crowds. Whether you're chasing sunrise over the Moray Firth, sampling world class single malts along the Speyside Whisky Trail, or spotting seals and dolphins in the North Sea, the NE250 packs in a little bit of everything.

It's a journey for those into history, nature lovers, foodies, and if you just love exploring a new road trip. Along the way, you'll find warm hospitality, charming accommodations, and more than enough scenic spots to pull over, breathe it all in, and remember why you came to Scotland in the first place.

Driving the NE250

The roads around the NE250 are generally easy to drive offering a mix of both two-way and some single track roads. Whilst navigating these narrow roads, you also need to prepared for sheep or deer who use the roads to get around.

In Scotland, we drive on the left and this is still the case on the single track roads. This can be very confusing/hazardous when moving between dual/single track roads, and it has been recommended by the local police to wear a band/bracelet on your wrist as a reminder of which side you should be on.

Passing places are used to allow traffic to pass on the single track roads, it is important to remember that these are passing places and not parking places. When driving on these roads, keep a "passing place" distance apart from the cars in front of you avoid congestion and pull in at the space at the side of the road to allow the oncoming traffic to pass you.

When it comes to the NE250, driving the route is half of the fun, with stunning coastal views, quaint fishing villages and beautiful wildlife to look out for. With all of this beauty to take in, it is especially important that you TAKE YOUR TIME.

Allow yourself to truly soak up the beauty of the land around you, coming to terms with how lucky we are to witness this heaven, rather than driving the NE250 to simply tick it off your bucket list.

Follow the highway code and park appropriately to maintain safety on the roads.

Shops and Fuel

When it comes to buying food and supplies around the NE250, there are a number of large, supermarkets spread along the route, in between which you will find smaller, local shops.

It is unlikely that you will find yourself short along the route, with the longest stretch without a supermarket being 45 miles between Fraserburgh and Buckie, however, there is a smaller Coop in between. In the Cairngorms National Park there are two supermarkets, one in Aviemore and one in Ballater. However, there is also a Co-op in Newtonmore and Granton-on-Spey if you find yourself needing supplies. It is also likely that you will find yourself tempted to eat out at many of the delicious cafes and restaurants around the route.

There are plenty of fuel stations that are quite evenly spread out along the NE250, however, you should know where each of them are to avoid running out of fuel on the road. We list all of the necessary fuel stations under each subsection of this book, and also detail their exact locations in our NE250 map that pairs with this book.

If you are travelling in a campervan or motorhome and require propane gas bottles, there are a number of retailers around the route selling Calor gas bottles which we detail on our map. If it is Flogas you require, you will be most likely to find stockists in Aberdeen, Peterhead and along the northern coastline. Aberdeen and Kinloss each have a station for refillable gas.

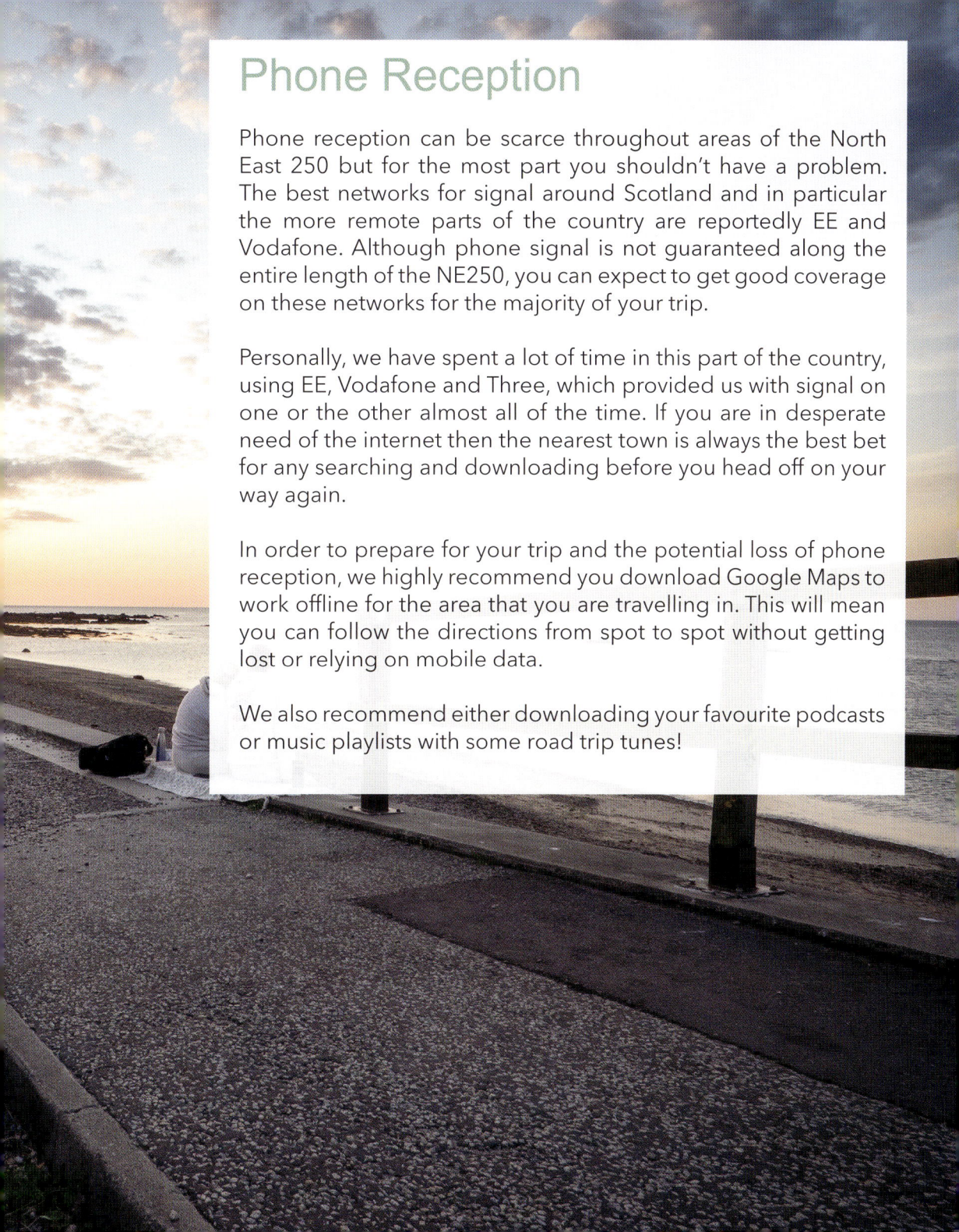

Phone Reception

Phone reception can be scarce throughout areas of the North East 250 but for the most part you shouldn't have a problem. The best networks for signal around Scotland and in particular the more remote parts of the country are reportedly EE and Vodafone. Although phone signal is not guaranteed along the entire length of the NE250, you can expect to get good coverage on these networks for the majority of your trip.

Personally, we have spent a lot of time in this part of the country, using EE, Vodafone and Three, which provided us with signal on one or the other almost all of the time. If you are in desperate need of the internet then the nearest town is always the best bet for any searching and downloading before you head off on your way again.

In order to prepare for your trip and the potential loss of phone reception, we highly recommend you download Google Maps to work offline for the area that you are travelling in. This will mean you can follow the directions from spot to spot without getting lost or relying on mobile data.

We also recommend either downloading your favourite podcasts or music playlists with some road trip tunes!

Weather in Scotland

It is fairly known that the weather in Scotland can be pretty temperamental. On average, the wettest parts of Scotland experience 5 rainy days a week, whilst the driest experience 3 days a week.

This means that choosing the right time for a road trip as epic as the NE250 requires some care and consideration.

As a general rule of thumb, the months of the year that experience the best weather in Scotland are April, May and June. These months tend to be drier, with cooler mornings and clearer skies than later in summer. As the summer months go on, the humidity returns to the air and the rainfall begins once again, with July and August tending to be much wetter.

The eastern coast of Scotland is known for its bitter wind chill so it is always worth bringing some warmer layers with you. In saying that, the eastern coast is also generally drier and gets more sunshine than the west coast.

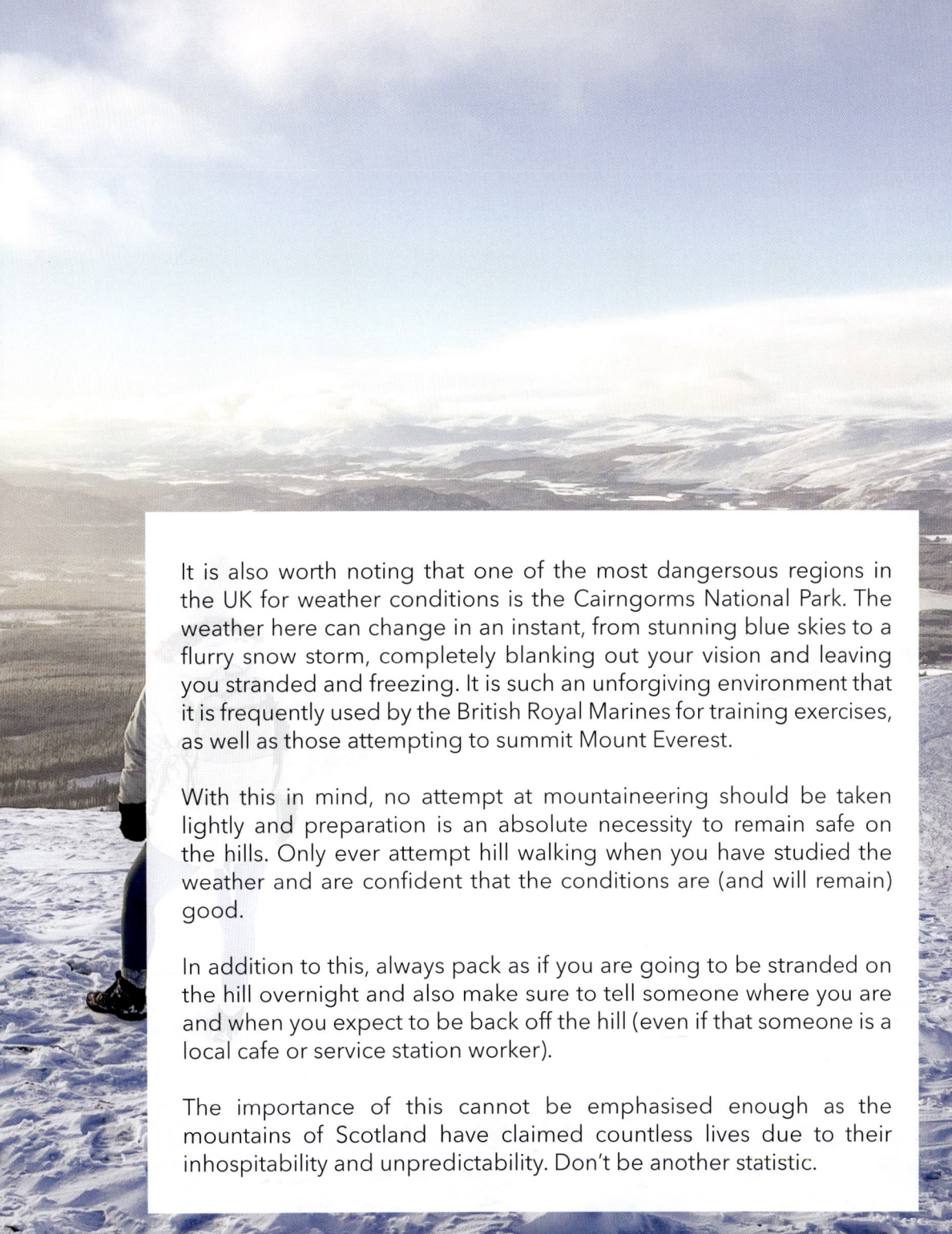

It is also worth noting that one of the most dangersous regions in the UK for weather conditions is the Cairngorms National Park. The weather here can change in an instant, from stunning blue skies to a flurry snow storm, completely blanking out your vision and leaving you stranded and freezing. It is such an unforgiving environment that it is frequently used by the British Royal Marines for training exercises, as well as those attempting to summit Mount Everest.

With this in mind, no attempt at mountaineering should be taken lightly and preparation is an absolute necessity to remain safe on the hills. Only ever attempt hill walking when you have studied the weather and are confident that the conditions are (and will remain) good.

In addition to this, always pack as if you are going to be stranded on the hill overnight and also make sure to tell someone where you are and when you expect to be back off the hill (even if that someone is a local cafe or service station worker).

The importance of this cannot be emphasised enough as the mountains of Scotland have claimed countless lives due to their inhospitability and unpredictability. Don't be another statistic.

How Long Should You Spend on the NE250?

This is everyone's first thought when it comes to planning an NE250 road trip, however, it is one without a real answer as it can really take however long you want it to.

There are people who only have a few days and want to make the most of their adventure and will pack in as many sights as they can in a day and others will travel at a more leisurely pace, making the most of their visit at each location and choosing to come back another time if they don't see it all. We all travel differently. However, to make it easier to plan your road trip we can give you an idea of how long SHOULD you spend on the NE250 and to that my answer is between 5-14 days.

Given that the road trip is only 250 miles, you could drive it relatively quickly and in 5 days you would still be able to see a lot. This would give you time to see the most beautiful coastal regions, as well as meander inland and explore the whisky trails and mountains of the Cairngorms.

In order to fully absorb the culture and history in this part of Scotland, I would suggest that you give yourself 7-14 days which will allow you to enjoy the beautiful walks, spend time exploring the incredible castles and enjoy eating out around the coastline.

If you do not have 7 days, you could always break this route up into sections and explore it when you can. The Cairngorms National Park and the northern coast of Moray are great areas to explore and make sure you save a day for the whisky trail!

The Rugged Side of the NE250

Steeped in centuries of history the North East 250 offers a journey through some of Scotland's most diverse landscapes and wild history. From the crashing waves and rugged sea cliffs of the Moray Firth coast to the rolling peaks of the Cairngorms, the route takes you through wild pine forests, windswept moorland, and glistening beaches where seals sunbathe and dolphins play in the sea.

This is a part of Scotland where ancient castles stand sentinel over the sea and whisky flows from distilleries along the Moray Whisky Trail.

It doesn't get much more soul stirring than the North East 250, a road trip that promises wild nature, historic charm, and the kind of peaceful seclusion that only the Scottish wilderness can offer.

34 Slains Castle

Wild Camping on the NE250

One of Scotland's greatest charms is the Right to Roam law, allowing all persons to venture where you please, as long as you do so respectfully. The Land Reform (Scotland) Act 2003 allows wild camping in Scotland opening the door to the glorious and desolate highlands that Scotland has to offer, and the beauty that lies there. There is honestly no better feeling than getting out into the open and being the only one for miles around.

There is a positive tolerance and understanding from the locals when it comes to wild camping in Scotland, that may be due to the understanding that it brings tourism and business. However, when you are looking for a spot to pitch up for the night, you cannot just choose anywhere you wish. Some people might not take too kindly to waking up to discover you pitched up in their back garden.

The rules we follow are as stated by the Outdoor Access Guidelines in Scotland

- Ensure you're out of sight of any residences, or at least 200m away from them.
- Choose a spot that isn't going to have people walking past your tent regularly.
- Camp away from towns and villages.
- Don't pitch up right beside a campsite, this is seen as quite rude. If you find an ideal spot, head around the corner out of sight of the campsite and you will be fine.
- Don't pitch up too many tents in a large group as this draws attention.
- Only drop grey waste and chemical toilet at designated areas.
- Take all your litter with you.
- Don't do the toilet near water, stay at least 30m away and bring a trowel to bury any evidence. Don't bury feminine hygiene products as these do not biodegrade.
- Use eco friendly soaps and detergents to protect the environment.
- Arrive after dark and leave before light. Do not overstay in one spot, or if you wish to use the same site make sure you leave and return to prevent the beauty of the highlands being ruined.
- When finished, leave the camping spot as you found it. There should be no evidence that you were there, apart from footprints and good memories!

Highland Bothies

When it comes to life on the wild side, the bothies of Scotland are about as wild as it gets. Nestled among the towering peaks of the Scottish Highlands surrounded by vast wilderness with nothing but the howling of the wind to keep you company, sleeping in
a bothy is perhaps one of the most unique experiences you will have in Scotland.

For those who have not heard of the term Bothy before, a Scottish Bothy is a small house (or hut) that sits in the most remote parts of the country. Once these huts would have been used as houses for farmers and shepherds, however, they have since fallen into ruin and been restored to a basic yet comfortable windproof and waterproof standard.

The idea behind the Scottish Bothy is to provide free shelter amongst one of the most dangerous and unforgiving environments on the planet. The huts are left unlocked and available for anyone and everyone to use as a place to rest for the night, sheltered from the harsh elements of the Scottish Highlands.

Bothies can be found across the length of Scotland, as well as in Wales and England, the vast majority of which are owned and maintained by the Mountain Bothy Association (MBA). This charity is responsible for the repair and upkeep around 100 bothies across the UK and is run by volunteers who love the wild side of the country so much they spend their weekends hiking across the land with the materials needed for the routine maintenance of the bothies.

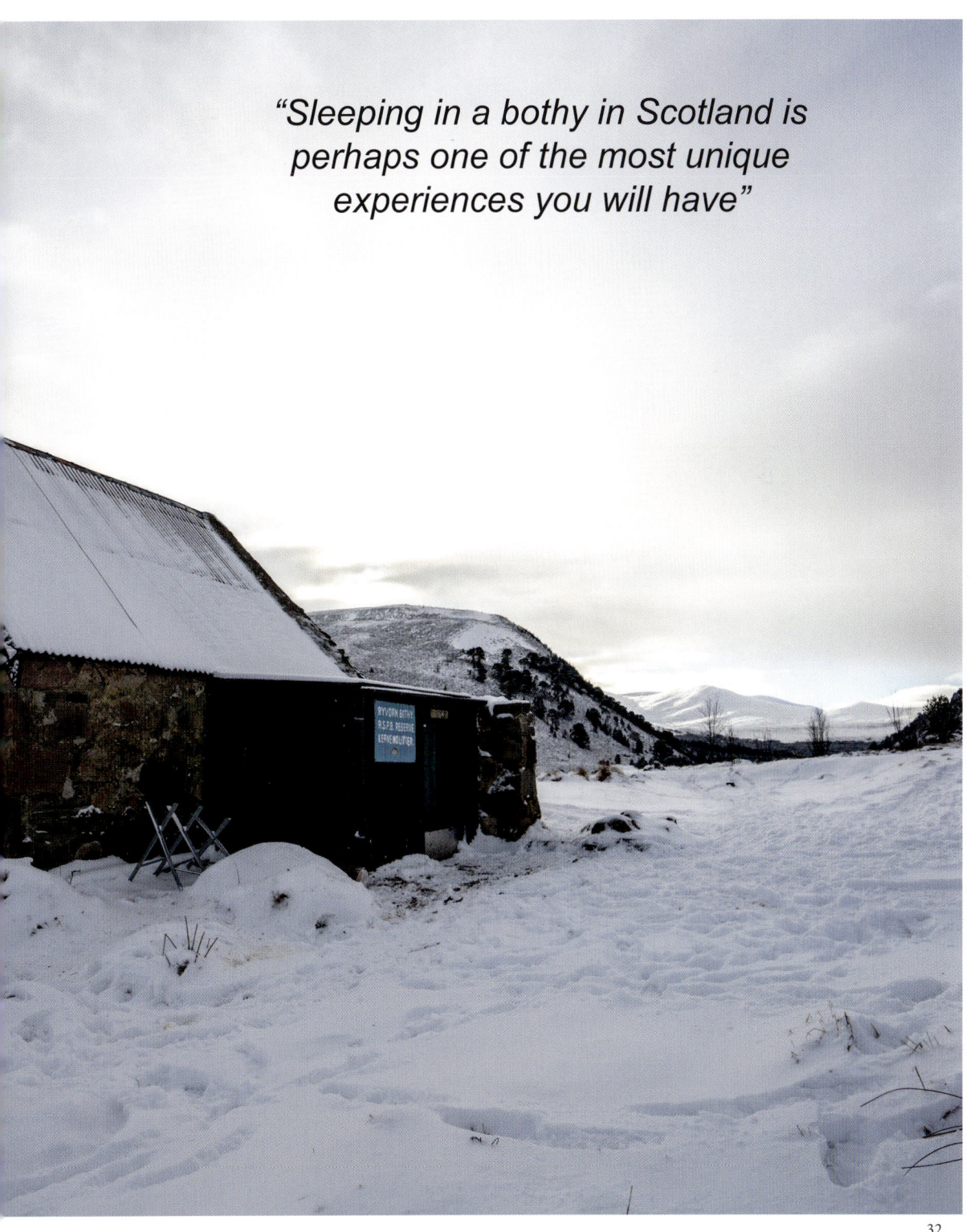

"Sleeping in a bothy in Scotland is perhaps one of the most unique experiences you will have"

Over the years, the MBA have come up with a set of guidelines for the use of Mountain Bothies that ensure the continued enjoyment and use of bothies for years to come.

- Bothies are used entirely at your own risk.
- Leave the bothy clean and tidy with dry kindling for the next visitors.
- Make other visitors welcome.
- Report any damage to whoever maintains the bothy.
- Avoid burying rubbish; this pollutes the environment.
- If there is no toilet at the bothy please bury human waste out of sight and well away from the water supply; never use the vicinity of the bothy as a toilet.
- Never cut live wood or damage estate property. Use fuel sparingly.
- Large groups and long stays are to be discouraged – bothies are intended for small groups on the move in the mountains.
- Because of overcrowding and lack of facilities, large groups (6 or more) should not use a bothy nor camp near a bothy without first seeking permission from the owner. Bothies are not available for commercial groups.

IMPORTANT NOTE - If you do plan on using a bothy, research the season availability of the bothies in each area. During specific seasons, such as the Grouse Shooting and Stag Stalking season of September to October, access restrictions to the mountains/estates in certain areas do apply.

Wild Swimming in Scotland

Wild swimming gives a sense of freedom and adventure. The icy cold water of Scotland's coast leaves you feeling alive and ready to face anything after a wee dook. Cold water can relax the body and eases muscle aches while boosting the immune system.

Swim with a partner for safety, and don't stay in until you're shivering, as this indicates the onset of hypothermia. Ensure you have warm layers to wear after swimming. It's also recommended to bring a hot water bottle or hot drink to warm up immediately after swimming, as hypothermia is a serious risk in Scotland.

Be aware that wild swimming is at your own risk. There are rarely any lifeguards on the beaches of Scotland and cold temperatures pose a genuine hypothermia risk. Research safe swimming practices, always swim with a partner, and bring a flotation aid.

91 Loch an Eilein Castle

Safety When Swimming

Growing in popularity, wild swimming has revealed several overlooked safety factors in Scotland, such as rip currents, cold shock, and after drop. To stay safe while wild swimming, familiarise yourself with these terms and effective ways to mitigate these dangers, as they can lead to fatal consequences if left unaddressed.

Rip currents: More relevant to seaside swimming, rip currents are the tidal pull that leaves the shoreline between the swells. Once caught in a rip current, it becomes challenging to swim against the water flow pulling you out to sea. To escape, swim parallel to the shoreline until you are out of the rip, then swim towards the shore.

Cramps: Extreme cold can cause cramps during wild swimming. Don't panic if you experience cramps in your legs or arms. Your body is naturally buoyant, so call for help while lying on your back with your ears in the water. This position allows you to balance and float easily until rescued or the cramp disappears.

After drop: This is the continuous decline of your internal body temperature after leaving the water. Don't wait until shivering to leave the water, as this indicates hypothermia has begun.

Cold shock: The involuntary gasp and muscle seizure experienced when entering cold water can lead to drowning or pneumonia if the head is submerged. Enter the water slowly and acclimatise before fully submerging.

Blood rush: After exiting the water, avoid jumping straight into a hot shower, as many cold-water swimmers end up fainting in the shower. The dilation of blood vessels in the outer extremities due to external water heat causes cold blood from arms and legs.

Saunas on the NE250

- Watershed Sauna, Findhorn
- Sauna at the Kings, Cullen
- Stravaig Saunas, Royal Deeside
- Driftwood, Stonehaven Paddleboarding
- Seabiscuit Sauna, Aberdeen

Best Places to Wild Swim on the NE250

Aberdeen Beach - Large and flat with gentle entry. Busy with passersby and surfers.

Stonehaven Beach - A popular stony beach with a cute seaside town.

Portsoy Tidal Pool - A tidal basin with easy entry and exit in the town of Portsoy.

Findhorn Beach - A huge stretch of stones and sand with a gentle entry. Try out Watershed Sauna after a dip.

Loch Morlich - A popular loch for watersports in the Cairngorm National Park

Loch Insh - With an onsite watersports centre, this is the perfect spot for a safe swim

Hiking on the NE250

Tracing a loop through some of Scotland's most varied terrain, the North East 250 offers an abundance of hiking opportunities for walkers of all abilities. From the heather-clad hills of the Cairngorms to the cliffside trails along the Moray Firth coast, the route is rich with trails that reward with incredible views.

The Cairngorms National Park has some of the most impressive mountain ranges you will find in Scotland and offers a chance to hike some of the highest peaks with the least amount of incline due to the height above sea level. It is essential that you are experienced and prepared before heading out into the hills however as the changes in weather can be sudden and it is incredibly dangerous.

One day you might find yourself weaving through the towering pine forests of Glenlivet, the next scaling windswept coastal paths near Pennan or Cullen with the sea crashing far below. Escape the hustle and bustle of the busy cities snd head out on the trails.

95 Meall a Bhuachaille

Please be aware that you will do this at your own risk.
Hiking in Scotland can be a dangerous activity, with unpredictable weather systems and an isolated and remote countryside. Before you leave on any hike it is recommended that you pack for bad weather, bring a map and compass, and let someone know where you are going.

Midges

If you are planning a trip to Scotland, you may have heard of the tiny beasties that are out to ruin your life and have the potential to ruin your holiday.. the midge. Midges have a wingspan 1-2mm and need blood to survive, therefore they have a pretty nasty bite which some people are more susceptible than others.

It might seem crazy to base an entire trip on the absence of some bugs, however, midges are a fierce, formidable force in the highlands that have driven the hardest of souls to tears.

When the midges wake up will be all dependent on the weather. Midges thrive in mild, damp weather so if the weather begins to heat up followed by some warm rain, the midges will tend to wake up when they have lots of water to lay their eggs in. If you are booking a trip to Scotland and want to completely avoid the midges then we would advise visiting Scotland outside of the summer months.

Midges don't like sun and wind so you may find them less likely to be out on a day where there is strong sunshine in Scotland (which can happen in summer would you believe) however they will start to come out during dawn and dusk and you can expect to see them on mild cloudy days too.

You can also check the midge forecast on Smidge so you can see what the midge situation is like in the place you are visiting.

Scan the QR code to head to our website where you can make sure you have all that you need to protect you from the midges.

Midge is pronounced "mid-jee"

Some tips for avoiding the midges

- Avoid damp areas such as lochs
- Head to higher ground
- Wear a midge net
- Fly nets – keep them closed
- Wear a midge repellent
- Wear a repelling bracelet
- Cover bare skin
- Incense sticks
- Citronella candles

An Lochan Uaine

4 Balmoral Castle & Pyramids

Responsibly Wild

The most beautiful part of the highlands of Scotland is due to how remote, rugged, and unforgiving the environment can be. The wilderness of the northern region of the UK has remained barren and uninhabited for hundreds, if not, thousands of years, far from the reach of the modern society.

With the blessing of the remote and untamable wilderness that can be found on the Isle of Skye comes with great responsibility to the increasing number of tourists who explore the route. A responsibility to admire, respect, and protect the beauty of this natural landscape.

Across Scotland, there are more and more spaces where wild camping has been made illegal, mainly due to the disrespect shown by the small minority of those camping who have abused this luxury and destroyed the environment.

No matter what wild activity you wish to partake in, the key message remains the same.

Leave No Trace.

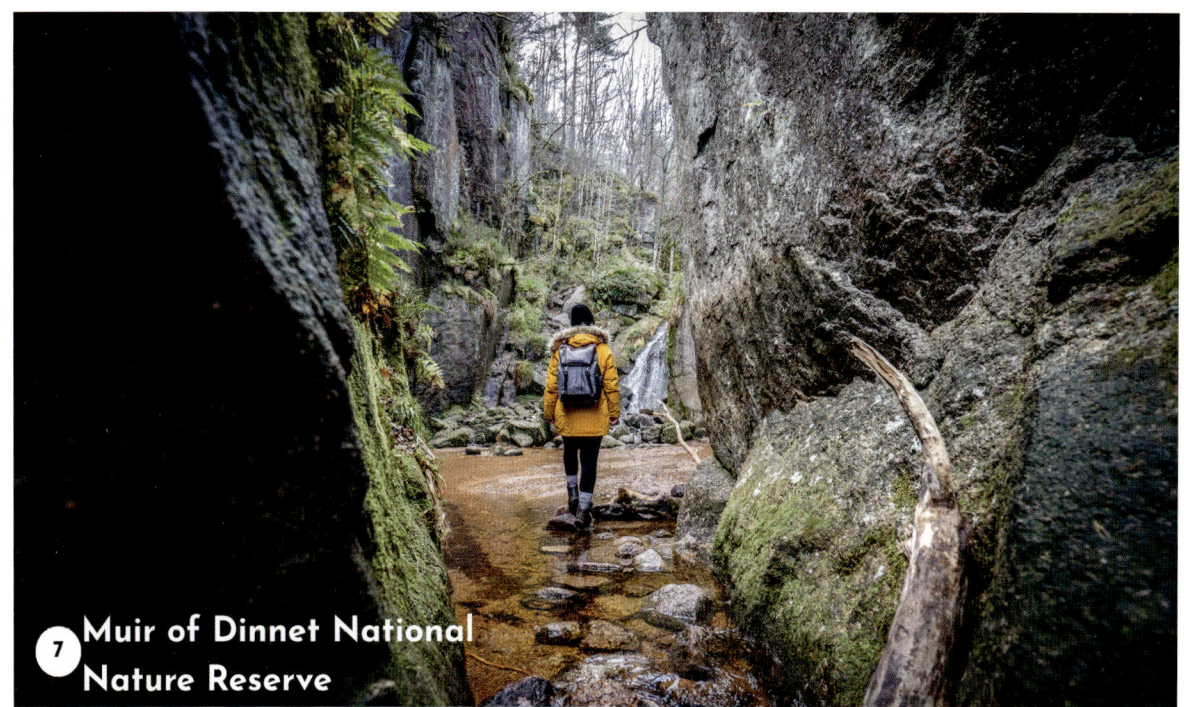

7 Muir of Dinnet National Nature Reserve

33 Collieston

Best of the NE250

In a world that rarely slows down, the North East 250 offers a welcome pause and a chance to reconnect with a side of Scotland that remains beautifully untamed. Skirting the rugged coastline of the Moray Firth, winding through the misty mountains of the Cairngorms, and meandering past fishing villages, ancient castles, and rolling farmland, the NE250 isn't just a road trip, it's a journey through the Scotland's hidden charm.

Unlike the raw and remote landscape of the far north, the NE250 is a more subtle storyteller where you will find a patchwork of powerful landscapes and rich heritage woven together with local warmth and hospitality. There are bustling harbour towns and peaceful glens, whisky trails filled with centuries of tradition, and quiet roads that reward every turn with a new perspective.

Although you are never too far from the comforts of modern life, the beauty of the NE250 lies in its balance with enough solitude to let your mind wander and more than enough beauty to keep your camera clicking.

It's recht fine tae ging awa
bit there's nithin like comin back
we unser the call o the land whisperin
ye've been awa too lang
mon hame quine
come awa ma loon
the North East is fa ye are
an we are
hame
tied igither fae mountain tae sea
we are the colour o autumn leaves
an athing in atween
we are rich in beauty

- Jo Gilbert, Spoken Word Artist & Poet

Read more of
Jo's work here

Best Distilleries to Visit on the NE250

- **The Macallan:** Known for its exceptional single malts and innovative architecture, the Macallan offers immersive experiences that delve into its rich heritage and whisky making process.
- **Glenfiddich:** As one of the few remaining family owned distilleries, Glenfiddich provides comprehensive tours showcasing its traditional methods and award winning whiskies.
- **Aberlour:** Situated in the heart of Speyside, Aberlour is celebrated for its rich and complex single malts, offering tastings that highlight its unique flavour profiles.
- **Glenfarclas:** This family run distillery has been here since 1836 and is renowned for its sherried whiskies. It offers tours that provide insights into its time honoured production techniques.
- **Benromach:** Located in Forres, Benromach combines traditional methods with a contemporary approach, producing distinctive single malts that reflect the character of Speyside.
- **Royal Lochnagar:** Found near Balmoral Castle, this distillery offers a glimpse into royal approved whisky production, with tours that explore its storied past and classic Highland malts.
- **Lost Loch Spirits:** Situated in Royal Deeside, Lost Loch Spirits is an award winning craft distillery offering micro tours and a unique Spirits School where visitors can distill their own personalised spirit.

Drink driving is illegal in Scotland. If you are driving around the NE250 then it is important to highlight that NO ALCOHOL should be consumed before driving in Scotland. Due to the low legal limit in Scotland, it is also recommended that you wait 24hrs after drinking before driving.

Best Distilleries & Breweries
on the NE250

Where better to indulge in Scotland's liquid gold than along the North East 250, the most densely populated whisky region in the world. This stretch of the country encompasses centuries of whisky tradition which offers a deliciously deep dive into Scotland's most cherished export.

The journey along the NE250 leads you through the heart of whisky country, where ancient distilleries sit close to rushing burns and within shadowy glens, many of which have been crafting single malts for over a hundred years. The best thing is that each distillery tells its own story, meaning there is always another one to visit. All distilleries must follow the strict rules of Scotch production, using only malted barley, water, and yeast, aged in oak for a minimum of three years.

The NE250 offers the perfect opportunity to explore a variety of distilleries, which is perfect for both whisky connoisseurs or those who are curious to try, from the globally acclaimed giants like The Macallan and Glenfiddich, to the smaller, characterful producers such as Benromach. Many offer tours that peel back the curtain on their processes, from maltings to stills, finishing in a tasting room to sample their finest products.

For those driving the route, you don't need to miss out as most distilleries offer take-home tasting kits so you can savour the experience at your leisure. There truly is no better way to connect with the spirit of Scotland than by sampling some whisky on the NE250.

Best Honesty Boxes and Farm Shops
on the NE250

Travelling the North East 250 is more than exploring the beautiful coastlines and historic castles, it's also a journey into Scotland's community-driven, countryside culture. One of the best ways to experience this is by visiting the many honesty boxes and farm shops around the region.

Honesty boxes are self service roadside stalls offering everything from fresh eggs and home baking to handmade crafts and produce, all operating on a simple system of trust, take what you like and leave the right amount of cash in the tin.

Some honesty boxes may have an option to bank transfer but it is always best to carry cash as most operate on this system.

Along the route you will also find traditional farm shops offering a wider selection of local goods, from artisan cheeses and meats to preserves and gifts, often with cafes or delis attached. Both offer an authentic taste of Aberdeenshire and Moray's rural life, and they're a great way to support small local businesses as you travel.

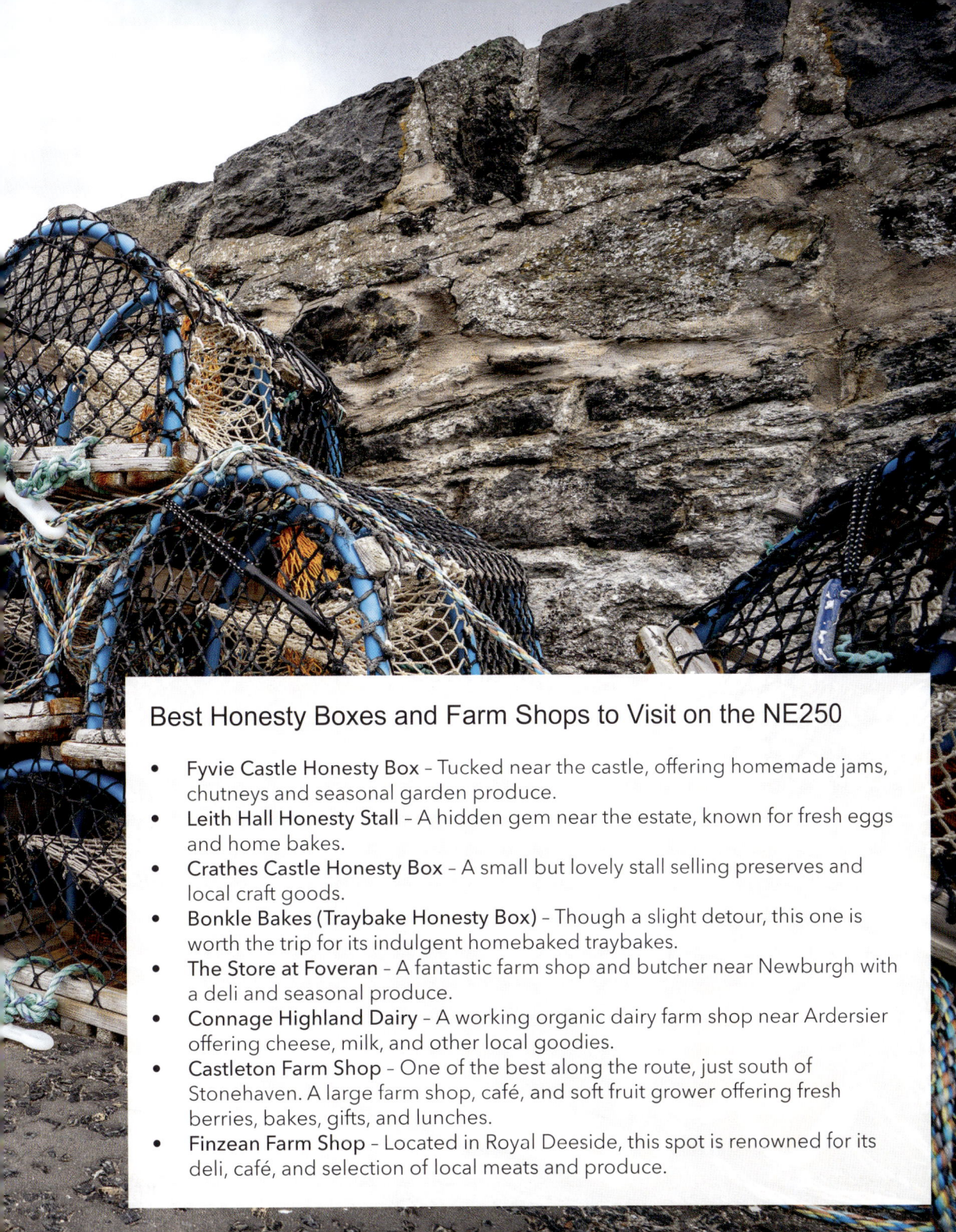

Best Honesty Boxes and Farm Shops to Visit on the NE250

- **Fyvie Castle Honesty Box** – Tucked near the castle, offering homemade jams, chutneys and seasonal garden produce.
- **Leith Hall Honesty Stall** – A hidden gem near the estate, known for fresh eggs and home bakes.
- **Crathes Castle Honesty Box** – A small but lovely stall selling preserves and local craft goods.
- **Bonkle Bakes (Traybake Honesty Box)** – Though a slight detour, this one is worth the trip for its indulgent homebaked traybakes.
- **The Store at Foveran** – A fantastic farm shop and butcher near Newburgh with a deli and seasonal produce.
- **Connage Highland Dairy** – A working organic dairy farm shop near Ardersier offering cheese, milk, and other local goodies.
- **Castleton Farm Shop** – One of the best along the route, just south of Stonehaven. A large farm shop, café, and soft fruit grower offering fresh berries, bakes, gifts, and lunches.
- **Finzean Farm Shop** – Located in Royal Deeside, this spot is renowned for its deli, café, and selection of local meats and produce.

Best Castles
on the NE250

The NE250 is often referred to as 'Scotland's Castle Country', and for good reason as nowhere else in the UK has such a high concentration of castles, ruins, and fortified manor houses.

With over 260 castles across the region, from coastal strongholds to regal estates nestled in wooded glens, there's no better place to dive into Scotland's rich and often turbulent history.

What makes Aberdeenshire's castles truly special is the diversity. Some, like the iconic Craigievar Castle, appear straight out of a fairy tale with their pink-hued walls and turrets. Others, such as Dunnottar, offer windswept drama, perched on the clifftop above the crashing North Sea.

There are royal residences such as Balmoral, which remains a private retreat for the British monarchy, and there are evocative ruins like Slains Castle, said to have inspired Bram Stoker's Dracula.

Visiting these castles is like leafing through the pages of Scotland's past, battles, betrayals, royal visits, and ghost stories. Many are beautifully preserved and offer guided tours, exhibitions, and lush gardens to explore. Others are remote and rugged, perfect for those who like to really imagine what life would have been like living there.

3 Braemar Castle

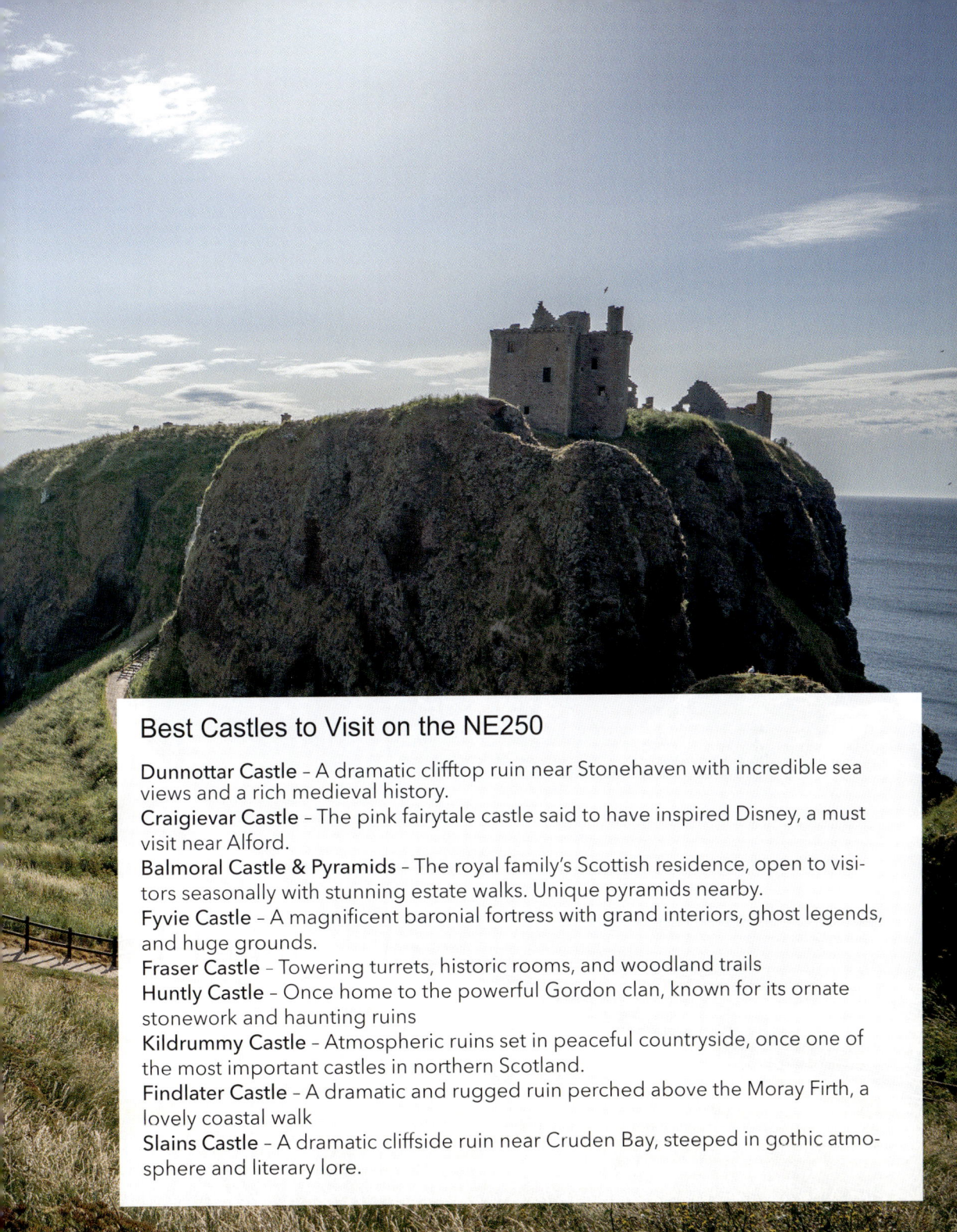

Best Castles to Visit on the NE250

Dunnottar Castle – A dramatic clifftop ruin near Stonehaven with incredible sea views and a rich medieval history.
Craigievar Castle – The pink fairytale castle said to have inspired Disney, a must visit near Alford.
Balmoral Castle & Pyramids – The royal family's Scottish residence, open to visitors seasonally with stunning estate walks. Unique pyramids nearby.
Fyvie Castle – A magnificent baronial fortress with grand interiors, ghost legends, and huge grounds.
Fraser Castle – Towering turrets, historic rooms, and woodland trails
Huntly Castle – Once home to the powerful Gordon clan, known for its ornate stonework and haunting ruins
Kildrummy Castle – Atmospheric ruins set in peaceful countryside, once one of the most important castles in northern Scotland.
Findlater Castle – A dramatic and rugged ruin perched above the Moray Firth, a lovely coastal walk
Slains Castle – A dramatic cliffside ruin near Cruden Bay, steeped in gothic atmosphere and literary lore.

Best Mountains to Visit on the NE250

- Ben Macdui (1,309m) – Scotland's second highest mountain, offering vast, windswept views across the Cairngorm plateau.
- Lochnagar (1,155m) – A challenging Munro near Balmoral, beloved by Queen Victoria and climbers alike.
- Mount Keen (939m) – The most easterly Munro. The ascent from Glen Esk via Glen Mark is the shortest route.
- Ben Rinnes (841m) – Towering over the Speyside whisky region it is the highest freestanding mountain in Moray.
- Meall a' Bhuachaille (810m) – A popular and photogenic ridge walk from Glenmore looking over Loch Morlich, ideal for sunrise or sunset.
- Morrone (859m) – Offering incredible views over Braemar and the Cairngorms, it's an underrated gem of a Corbett and the only significant mountain climb in Scotland to start from the centre of a village.
- Tap o' Noth (563m) – A shorter hike with a fascinating Iron Age hill fort at the summit with views across to Ben Rinnes on a clear day. This is the second highest hillfort in Scotland.
- Scolty Hill (299m) – A family-friendly hike near Banchory, topped with a commemorative tower and great views.

Best Mountains
on the NE250

The story of Scotland's northeast coast and the mighty Cairngorm Mountains is one carved from ancient forces and timeless natural beauty.

Roughly 400 million years ago, during the aftermath of the Caledonian Mountain-building Event, the eastern side of Scotland rose up into a formidable landscape of towering peaks and rolling highlands. Over millions of years, nature continued to sculpt and refine the land. Ice ages came and went, each glaciation grinding and polishing the mountains, gouging out deep valleys and corries that cradle lochs and forests today.

These glacial movements gave the Cairngorms their distinctive rounded summits and wide open plateaus, creating one of the most unique mountain environments in Britain, a true Arctic wilderness in the heart of Scotland.

As you move from the heights of the Cairngorms to the sea-sprayed shores of the Moray Firth, the scenery tells a tale of constant transformation, a land where raw geological power and centuries of human history coexist in perfect harmony.

Today, the Cairngorms and the NE250 offer you a chance to step into this ancient world, to breathe the pure air, feel the vastness of the landscape, and find the kind of peace and wonder that only a place as timeless as this can provide.

The beauty you see before you has been hundreds of millions of years in the making. Now it waits for you, to explore, to experience, and to remember forever.

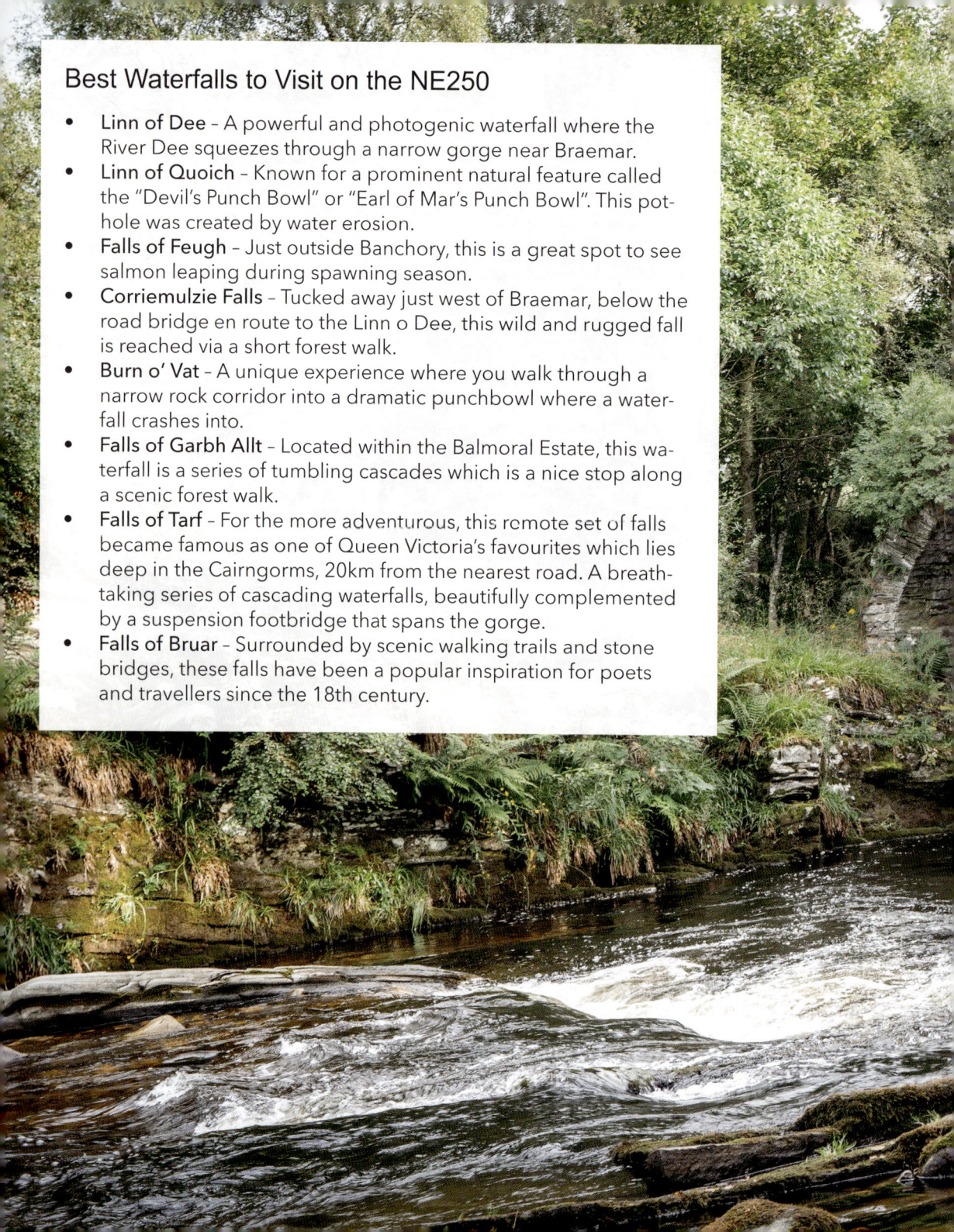

Best Waterfalls to Visit on the NE250

- **Linn of Dee** - A powerful and photogenic waterfall where the River Dee squeezes through a narrow gorge near Braemar.
- **Linn of Quoich** - Known for a prominent natural feature called the "Devil's Punch Bowl" or "Earl of Mar's Punch Bowl". This pothole was created by water erosion.
- **Falls of Feugh** - Just outside Banchory, this is a great spot to see salmon leaping during spawning season.
- **Corriemulzie Falls** - Tucked away just west of Braemar, below the road bridge en route to the Linn o Dee, this wild and rugged fall is reached via a short forest walk.
- **Burn o' Vat** - A unique experience where you walk through a narrow rock corridor into a dramatic punchbowl where a waterfall crashes into.
- **Falls of Garbh Allt** - Located within the Balmoral Estate, this waterfall is a series of tumbling cascades which is a nice stop along a scenic forest walk.
- **Falls of Tarf** - For the more adventurous, this remote set of falls became famous as one of Queen Victoria's favourites which lies deep in the Cairngorms, 20km from the nearest road. A breathtaking series of cascading waterfalls, beautifully complemented by a suspension footbridge that spans the gorge.
- **Falls of Bruar** - Surrounded by scenic walking trails and stone bridges, these falls have been a popular inspiration for poets and travellers since the 18th century.

Best Waterfalls
on the NE250

The northeast of Scotland, including the NE250 route, is a region renowned for its beautiful landscapes and unpredictable weather. While the Scottish highlands are famous for their frequent rainfall, the northeast enjoys a climate that can shift rapidly, with rain often making an appearance just when you least expect it. This ever changing weather contributes to the lush green scenery that defines much of the area, supporting diverse ecosystems and some of the most captivating natural beauty in the country.

The abundant rainfall nurtures the rich landscapes and is the perfect setting for an abundance of stunning waterfalls. Along the NE250, you'll encounter numerous waterfalls, each one adding to the region's peaceful atmosphere and offering a glimpse into the power of nature at its finest.

Many waterfalls in the area are easily accessible with marked walking paths, while others require a little more effort to enjoy. The main thing is that all reward visitors with a moment of calm and a deep connection to the untamed Scottish landscape. They are especially dramatic after rain, so keep your waterproofs handy and your camera ready.

Falls of Truim

Best Beaches
on the NE250

Stretching along the rugged coastlines of Aberdeenshire and Moray, the NE250 is home to some of the most beautiful golden, unspoiled beaches in Scotland.

From the wild, windswept sands of the North Sea to secluded coves sheltered between cliffs, you are bound to find something to suit your fancy.

Picture golden sands that stretch endlessly, inviting waves for a wee dook (if you are brave enough), or hidden spots where the only footprints are your own. Many of the beautiful beaches are backed by towering dunes and decorated with swaying machar grass, painting a post card worthy scene.

While some of the beaches around the NE250 may feel remote and untouched, others are bordered by charming villages with warm, local hospitality. If you stumble upon a beach that's too busy for your taste, simply turn the corner or follow the coastline to find another peaceful spot.

The clear water can be tempting for a chilly dook on a cold day, it may look tropical but it certainly takes a few deep breaths before you duck under.

NOTE - A blue flag beach in Scotland is an award given to beaches that meet high standards of water quality and safety. There are several of these along the NE250.

Best Beaches to Visit on the NE250

- **Balmedie Beach** – Expansive golden sands backed by dunes, perfect for long walks and close to Aberdeen.
- **St Cyrus Beach** – Located within St. Cyrus National Nature Reserve, a wide stretch of sand surrounded by dramatic cliffs. Fantastic wildlife-watching opportunities.
- **Newburgh Seal Beach** – Known for its seal colony and a peaceful walk along the dunes.
- **Cruden Bay** – A beautiful beach overlooked by the ruins of Slains Castle, a fascinating ruin said to have inspired Dracula.
- **Fraserburgh Beach** – A great family friendly spot where the Moray Firth meets the North Sea with a long promenade and great views across the bay.
- **Rosehearty Beach** – A sheltered spot perfect for a quiet paddle or picnic. Great overnight parking at the Rosehearty Boat Club.
- **Cullen Beach (Blue Flag)** – A long beach near the famous Cullen viaduct and the birthplace of the well known Cullen Skink.
- **Findhorn Beach (Blue Flag)** – A perfect spot for sunset views, birdwatching, and peaceful seaside moments.

Best Walking Trails
on the NE250

Scotland's landscapes are a hiker's paradise, and the NE250 route offers some of the most diverse and breathtaking walks you'll find anywhere in the country. There are numerous coastal paths with dramatic sea views as well as an abundance of forest trails that lead you deep into the heart of the Cairngorms.

As well as the low level, short, leisurely walks, there are a number of steeper hills in the area, including some munros which we have included in our best mountains section.

This region of Scotland is also home to many multi-day walks which give you the opportunity to experience Scotland's rich history and culture, passing by ancient castles, battlefields, and monuments along the way.

If you don't fancy hiking over multiple days, it is also possible to do some of these walks in sections.

The Deeside Way

The Deeside Way is a 66km (41mile) long distance trail that follows the route of the old Royal Deeside Railway from the heart of Aberdeen all the way to Ballater in the Cairngorms National Park. This walk is ideal for walkers or cyclists and offers a scenic route with a gentle gradient and well maintained path that winds through charming towns like Banchory, Aboyne, and Dinnet, passing woodland, farmland, and riverside views along the way. The trail also passes historic railway stations, viaducts, and old railway lines dotted along the route.

The Moray Coast Trail

The Moray Coast Trail is a beautiful route spanning 80km (50 miles) stretching from Forres to Cullen which is often described as one of Scotland's most beautiful coastal walks. The walk underfoot is a mix of pavements, gravel paths, grassy tracks, and beach sections and passes through picturesque villages such as Findhorn, Burghead, Hopeman, Lossiemouth, Buckie, Portknockie, and Cullen.

Bennachie

Dominating the skyline of Aberdeenshire, Bennachie is one of Scotland's most iconic and beloved hill ranges. The range isn't especially high by Scottish standards, but its compact and relatively straightforward.

The most recognisable summit is Mither Tap (518m), crowned with the remains of an ancient Pictish hillfort you will be rewarded with sweeping views over the countryside, towards the Cairngorms in one direction and out to the Moray Firth in the other. The highest point of the range is Oxen Craig (528m), which is slightly further west and quieter than Mither Tap, but equally rewarding.

There are multiple waymarked trails starting from both the Bennachie Visitor Centre (near Chapel of Garioch) and the Rowantree and Back O' Bennachie car parks, ranging from gentle forest strolls to steep scrambles. Popular routes include the Mither Tap Trail, the Colony Trail (passing the remains of a 19th-century crofting settlement), and the longer Gordon Way, which connects the Bennachie hills with nearby Suie and Clatt.

The Speyside Way

The Speyside Way is one of Scotland's Great Trails, a long distance route covering 105km (65 miles) blending stunning Highland landscapes with rich cultural heritage, whisky distilleries, and small villages. Starting at the fishing town of Buckie on the Moray Firth coast, the trail gently follows the course of the River Spey, one of the UK's fastest flowing rivers, south through the heart of Speyside whisky country, finishing in Aviemore, on the edge of the Cairngorms National Park. It is often completed in 5-8 days however it is also possible to do short sections of the walk.

The terrain is largely gentle, with sections along old railway lines, forest tracks, riverside paths, and quiet roads, making it ideal for both day walkers and those looking for an accessible multi-day trek.

The trail is well waymarked, and there's ample accommodation ranging from cosy B&Bs to wild camping spots. Cyclists can also enjoy large portions of the route, particularly between Fochabers and Ballindalloch.

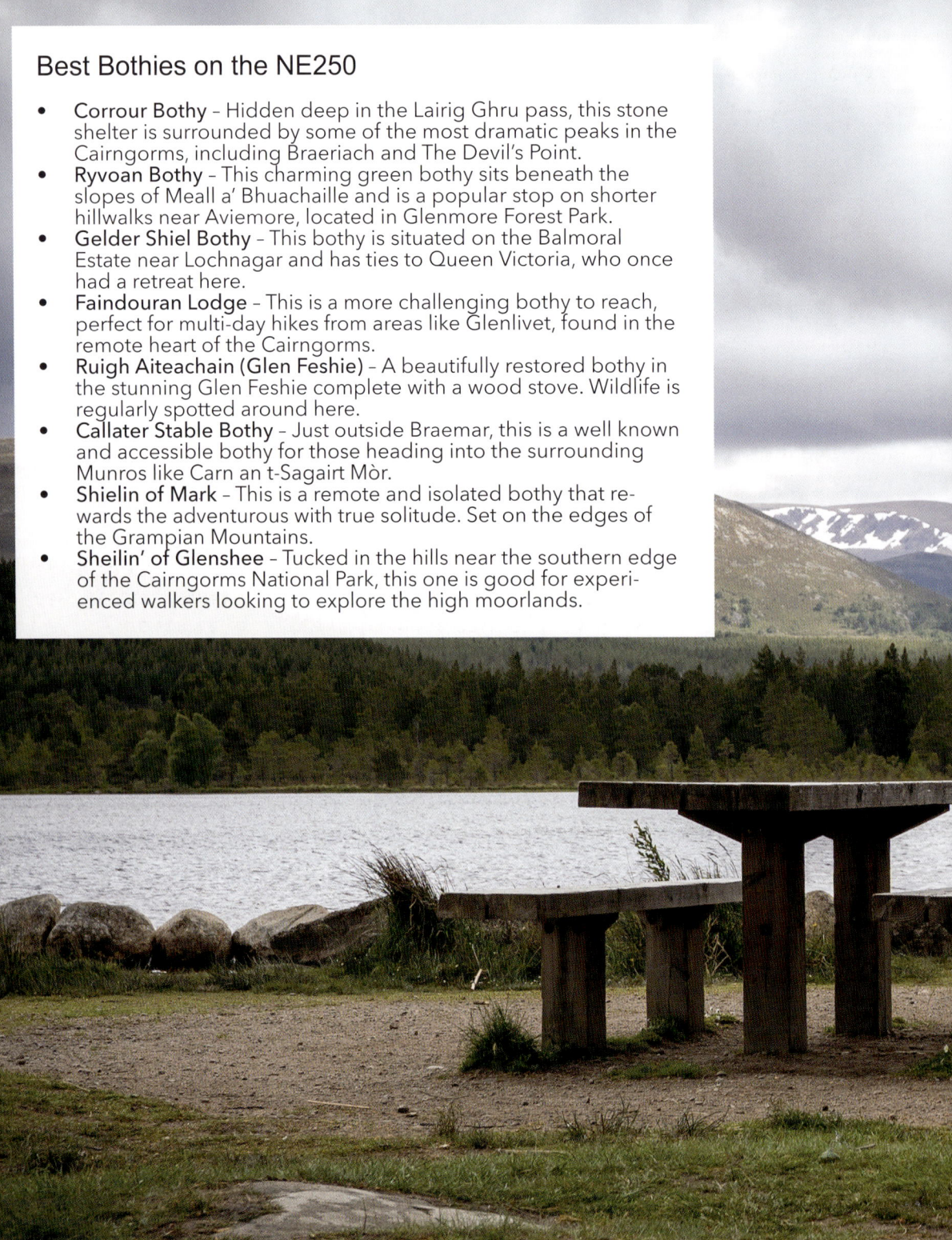

Best Bothies on the NE250

- **Corrour Bothy** – Hidden deep in the Lairig Ghru pass, this stone shelter is surrounded by some of the most dramatic peaks in the Cairngorms, including Braeriach and The Devil's Point.
- **Ryvoan Bothy** – This charming green bothy sits beneath the slopes of Meall a' Bhuachaille and is a popular stop on shorter hillwalks near Aviemore, located in Glenmore Forest Park.
- **Gelder Shiel Bothy** – This bothy is situated on the Balmoral Estate near Lochnagar and has ties to Queen Victoria, who once had a retreat here.
- **Faindouran Lodge** – This is a more challenging bothy to reach, perfect for multi-day hikes from areas like Glenlivet, found in the remote heart of the Cairngorms.
- **Ruigh Aiteachain (Glen Feshie)** – A beautifully restored bothy in the stunning Glen Feshie complete with a wood stove. Wildlife is regularly spotted around here.
- **Callater Stable Bothy** – Just outside Braemar, this is a well known and accessible bothy for those heading into the surrounding Munros like Carn an t-Sagairt Mòr.
- **Shielin of Mark** – This is a remote and isolated bothy that rewards the adventurous with true solitude. Set on the edges of the Grampian Mountains.
- **Sheilin' of Glenshee** – Tucked in the hills near the southern edge of the Cairngorms National Park, this one is good for experienced walkers looking to explore the high moorlands.

Best Bothies
on the NE250

Bothies offer a truly unique way to experience the remoteness and beauty of the region. These simple, often stone built shelters are free to use and maintained by the Mountain Bothies Association (MBA), providing basic refuge for hikers, cyclists, and adventurers exploring the great outdoors. If you do use them, it is great to donate and give back.

While the NE250 itself is primarily a driving route, it passes close to a number of bothies in the region, perfect if you are planning some walks detouring into the hills or incorporating into a longer hiking adventure.

These bothies are not only a shelter from the storm, but a doorway into a slower, more immersive way of travelling and one that puts you right at the heart of Scotland's raw and rugged landscapes.

Remember, bothies operate on a first-come, first-served basis and if you use it you are expected to follow the Bothy Code: leave no trace, respect others, and appreciate the wildness they offer. We like to carry a tent when we go on bothy adventures, just in case the bothy is full on our arrival (which has happened on a number of occassions).

Best Aires
on the NE250

An overnight motorhome aire is a designated area where campervans and motorhomes can park for a short stay, typically one night. These aires often provide basic amenities such as fresh water, waste disposal, and sometimes electricity, offering a convenient and cost effective alternative to traditional campsites. They are usually situated near towns or attractions, allowing us to explore local areas easily.

In response to the increasing popularity of motorhome tourism, Moray Council has initiated a consultation to manage overnight stays for campervans and motorhomes at designated council owned locations. Provisional sites have been identified in areas including Lossiemouth, Cullen, Buckie, Forres, Portgordon, Burghead, Ballindalloch, Craigellachie, and Aberlour. This initiative aims to support sustainable tourism while addressing community concerns about unmanaged overnight parking.

By providing structured overnight parking options, Moray Council seeks to enhance the experience for visitors and residents alike, ensuring that the region remains welcoming and accessible to motorhome travellers.

Best Aires to Stay at on the NE250

- **Glenbuchty Stopover Motorhome Aire** – A peaceful five pitch stopover with sea views, hardstanding, waste service (£5), and year-round access for £5 per night.
- **Arnbath Stopover Motorhome Aire** – A stunning two pitch retreat near Portsoy with breathtaking sea views and dark skies, £15 per night, open all year.
- **Rosehearty Boat Club** – A spacious seafront field with fresh water, waste disposal, and electric hook-up from £10 to £15 per night; cash only.
- **Cruden Bay / Port Erroll Harbour** – A quiet coastal stop with fresh water and toilets, donation based overnight stay, perfect for vans up to 7m.
- **Lossiemouth East Beach Car Park** – A relaxed beachfront parking spot with bins and a donation box; ideal for a one-night seaside stay.
- **Nairn Harbour** – Scenic harbour-side bays with fresh water and £10 overnight parking; dogs welcome and open year round.
- **Findhorn West Beach Motorhome Stopover** – A beachside aire with toilets, waste services, and secure entry; £17 per night, booking essential.
- **Cullen Motorhome Stopover** – A prime coastal location for self-contained vans at £10 per night (or £15 in peak season); online booking required.

54 Bow Fiddle Rock

SIGHTS

Walks 1. Callater Stable Walkers' Bothy

Towns 2. Braemar

Castles & Historical Sights
3. Braemar Castle
4. Balmoral Castle & Pyramids
5. Corgarff Castle
6. Lecht Mine
8. Tomnaverie Stone Circle
9. Kildrummy Castle
11. Craigievar Castle
12. Castle Fraser, Garden & Estate
13. Crathes Castle
14. Drum Castle - Garden & Estate
15. Dunnottar Castle

Nature Spots 7. Muir of Dinnet National Nature Reserve

Waterfalls 10. Dess Waterfall

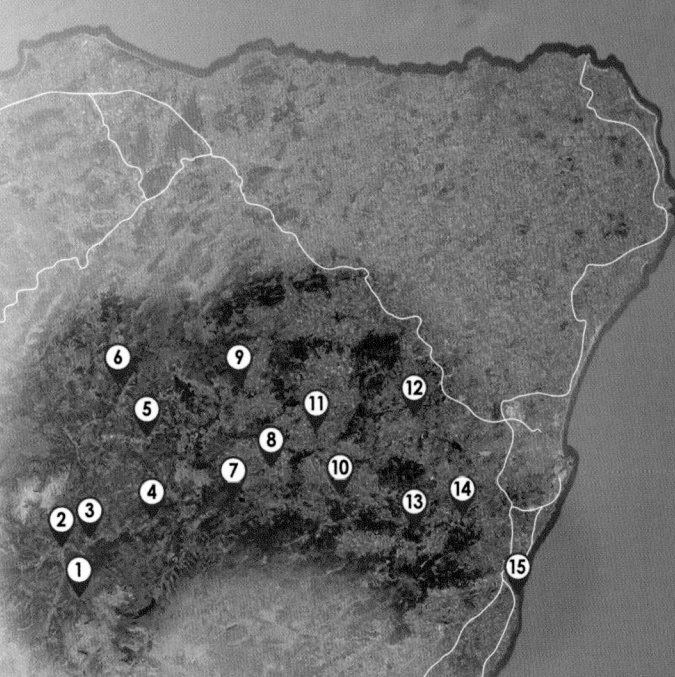

Braemar & Royal Deeside

As you head east from the heart of the Cairngorms, you'll find yourself on one of Scotland's most scenic and peaceful routes – Royal Deeside. Following the River Dee, this beautiful glen is full of stunning views, charming villages, and a real sense of history. The road leads you from the rugged hills around Braemar to the vibrant city of Aberdeen, with plenty of spots to explore along the way.

Royal Deeside is known for its royal connections, with Queen Victoria famously falling in love with the area back in the 1800s. Her influence is still felt today, especially around Balmoral, the royal family's Scottish retreat. You'll find lovely castles like Craigievar, with its fairytale turrets, and Kildrummy, with its atmospheric ruins, dotting the landscape. These historic places give a glimpse into the area's rich past, full of stories about kings, queens, and battles.

But it's not just the history that makes Royal Deeside so special, the scenery here is also absolutely breathtaking. In autumn, the forests glow with golden light. In summer, the hills are covered in purple heather and the River Dee sparkles as it winds through the glen, offering peaceful spots to stop and enjoy the surroundings.

As you approach Aberdeen, the wildness of the Highlands begins to soften into the rolling hills and farmland of the east. But even as you leave the mountains behind, the magic of Royal Deeside stays with you. It's a place that's peaceful, grand, and filled with stories waiting to be discovered.

Take a little time to wander through Braemar, visit Balmoral if you can, and explore the lovely village of Ballater. There's something about the charm of this area that will make you want to slow down, breathe in the fresh air, and enjoy every moment of your journey. It's a place that always leaves us wanting to return again and again.

2 Braemar

1. Callater Stable Walkers' Bothy

Callater Stable Walkers' Bothy is a remote and well loved stop just south of Braemar, perched at the head of Loch Callater in a dramatic glen, surrounded by towering Munros. It's a popular bothy for those tackling the likes of Carn an t-Sagairt Mòr, Carn a' Choire Bhoidheach, and the mighty Lochnagar. The approach follows a rough track from Braemar, making it a relatively accessible bothy for a day walk or an overnight adventure. Inside, it's simple yet atmospheric, with stone walls, wooden beams, and a steady stream of visitors who often leave notes and stories in the bothy book.

-> Follow the trail from Linn of Dee car park for about 7 miles through Glen Dee. ///blindfold.scorecard.unscrew

2. Braemar

Tucked away in the heart of the Cairngorms National Park is Braemar, a charming Highland village steeped in history, surrounded by dramatic mountain scenery and packed with character.

The village is best known for hosting the world-famous Braemar Gathering since the 1830's which is attended regularly by the Royal Family and held annually on the first Saturday of September. It features traditional events like caber tossing, tug o' war, and Highland dancing, alongside pipe bands and athletic competitions.

-> Parking available in town centre, along with public toilets. Wheelchair accessible. ///ribs.hiker.lakes

3. Braemar Castle

Braemar Castle is located near the village of Braemar and is open to the public Wednesday-Sunday. The grounds were first built in the 11th century, however the castle we see today was constructed in 1628 by John Erskine and has since been a hunting lodge, fortress, garrison and family home.

Braemar is the only castle in the UK which is under community management, therefore funds raised go towards preserving the castle. Unfortunately, due to steep winding staircases a tour of the building is not suitable for those with impaired mobility. There is a small car park and a short walk towards the castle grounds. Cost of entry is adult - £16 and a child is £8.

-> Dogs are welcome on the grounds but not inside the castle. The castle offers guided tours. Large car park also available. The grounds are wheelchair accessible. ///albatross.paddle.theory

3 Braemar Castle

4. Balmoral Castle & Pyramids

Balmoral Castle is located in the heart of the Cairngorms and has been the Scottish Highland retreat of the British royal family since 1852. The castle is open to the public from April through to August when visitors can explore the castle grounds, gardens, and exhibitions daily from 10.00am - 5.00pm.

While the castle is a private residence, the public can visit the ballroom, which hosts exhibitions showcasing the castle's rich history and royal connections. The estate also features a cafe serving local produce and a gift shop offering Scottish and royal themed souvenirs.

Admission is £18.50 for adults, £9.50 for children. The grounds are dog-friendly, provided dogs are kept on a lead.

-> *Dogs are permitted in the grounds but not inside buildings. Accessibility features are in place for the grounds, though interior access may be limited. ///pest.tonight.flattery*

The Balmoral Pyramid, also known as Prince Alberts Cairn, is one of the 11 pyramids that sit hidden amongst the forest of the Balmoral Estate near Balmoral Castle. The largest of them all is Prince Alberts Cairn which was constructed after his death in 1861 as a symbol of Queen Victoria's love for him.

The other 10 cairns in the Balmoral Estate commemorate the marriages of Queen Victoria's children. This structure is a popular site to visit whilst walking in the Cairngorms National Park due to the pleasant walk and fantastic views from the top.

Paid parking is available at Crathie Tourist Information and there are two walking options to get there.

-> *Park at Crathie car park near Balmoral, cross the bridge, walk about 800 metres along the road, then follow the forest trail for around 1km to reach the Balmoral Pyramid. Hike to the pyramids is quite steep across mud terrain. ///costly.champions.minivans*

4 Balmoral Castle & Pyramids

5. Corgarff Castle

Corgarff Castle is an impressive, white washed tower house set against the rugged backdrop of the Cairngorms. Originally built in the 16th century, it has a very turbulent history of clan feuds, including the Jacobite uprisings, and military occupation. Its distinctive star shaped perimeter wall was added when it became a Redcoat garrison, keeping watch over this remote landscape.

The castle is managed today by Historic Environment Scotland and tickets are available to buy and explore the castle. It is cheaper to buy tickets online, adult £7.50 and child £4.50.

-> Dogs are welcome in the grounds but not inside. The castle has some accessibility features. No on-site Wi-Fi. ///young.crash.stability

6. Lecht Mine

Once a busy centre for iron and manganese mining in the 18th and 19th centuries, today it's a quiet, atmospheric place to explore. The restored red roofed crushing plant stands out against the wild moorland whilst also offering a glimpse into Scotland's industrial past. Information boards explain the mine's history and the harsh conditions workers faced here. The site is easily accessible via a short walk from the roadside, with beautiful views over the surrounding hills.

-> Park at the Well of Lecht car park on the A939 between Tomintoul and the Lecht Ski Centre, then follow the signposted track north for approximately 800 metres. Dog-friendly but involves rough terrain. ///welcome.scoping.science

7. Muir of Dinnet National Nature Reserve

Muir of Dinnet National Nature Reserve is located near Ballatar within the Cairngorms National Park. It is a stunning landscape of woodlands, wetlands, and heather moorland and home to the famous Burn O'Vat, a giant glacial pothole carved out during the last Ice Age, where you can discover a hidden waterfall by stepping through a narrow rock passage.

Starting from the Burn O'Vat Visitor Centre, four waymarked trails range from just under a mile to nearly four miles, including the scenic Loch Kinord circular. The visitor centre itself is open daily from 10am–4pm (Easter to October) and features interactive displays, touch tables, and a model of the reserve to help plan your route, along with picnic benches and accessible facilities.

Motorhomes and campervans that are self-contained can Stay the Night in the main car park, with space for up to six vehicles (under 6m), and there is a suggested donation of £10. The site offers chemical toilet disposal (suggested £5 donation), but no grey waste, electricity or water. Accessible all year round, with surfaced paths to picnic benches and rest areas throughout.

-> Dogs are welcome but should be kept under control to protect wildlife. The reserve has paths that may be suitable for some visitors with mobility challenges, but facilities are limited. Access to the Muir of Dinnet itself is not accessible and invloves climbing. ///lends.chicken.slide

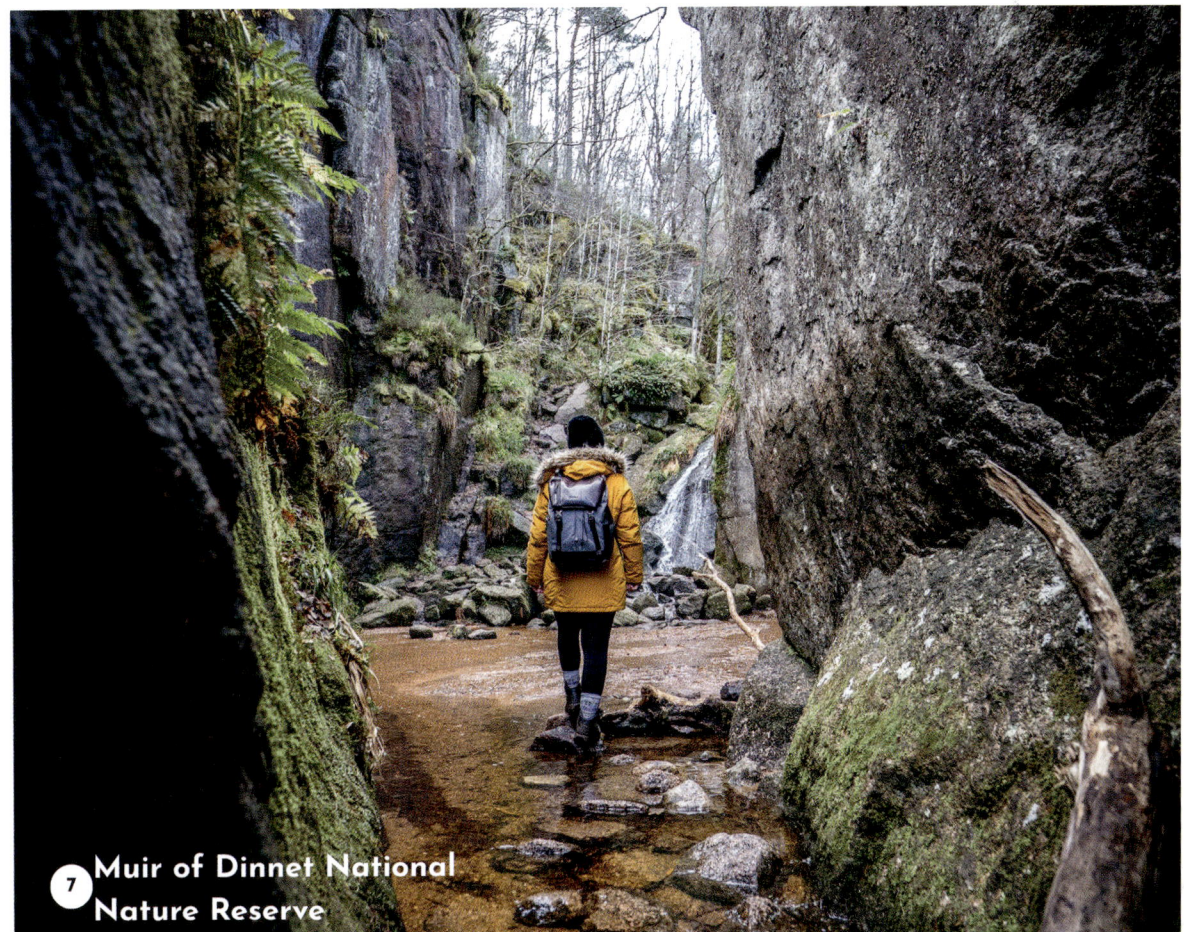

7 Muir of Dinnet National Nature Reserve

8. Tomnaverie Stone Circle

Tomnaverie Stone Circle is one of many stone circles unique to north eastern Scotland. This ancient flat lying stone circle located near Tarland dates back over 4,500 years to the Neolithic period and was likely used until AD 1600s, it is now managed by Historic Scotland. The large recumbent stone is flanked by two upright pillars, with smaller stones forming a circle around a central cairn. Lochnagar is a prominent mountain to the south west and it is believed that Tomnaverie Stone Circle was positioned to align with the moon at key times of the year.

From the car park it is only a 5 minute walk up the hill with great views to the standing stones. If you walk beyond the stone circle there is the Royal Observer Corps Nuclear Bunker which was built during the Cold War to monitor the location and strength of possible nuclear strikes.

-> Park at the small car park just off the B9094 near Tarland, then follow the signposted uphill path for approximately 300 metres to the site. Open to the public and dog-friendly; however, there are no facilities on-site. ///scarves.reports.jubilant

9. Kildrummy Castle

Kildrummy Castle stands as one of eastern Scotland's most extensive 13th-century castle ruins. Once the formidable seat of the Earls of Mar, its design includes a distinctive shield shaped layout, curtain walls, and multiple towers, notably the Snow Tower. Throughout its history, the castle has witnessed significant events, including sieges during the Wars of Scottish Independence and involvement in the Jacobite Rising of 1715.

Today, the castle is managed by Historic Environment Scotland and is open to explore the castle's ruins and the surrounding gardens. It is open from April - September on weekdays. Admission prices are £8.50 for adults, £5.00 for children and Historic Environment Scotland members go free.

-> Managed by Historic Environment Scotland, dogs on leads are welcome in outdoor areas. The site has uneven terrain, which may pose challenges for accessibility. ///predict.backdrop.hides

10. Dess Waterfall

Dess Waterfall, is a secluded, picturesque waterfall on the River Dee nestled within lush woodland near Aboyne. Dess Waterfall is surrounded by woodland and is a beautiful place to walk to. It is accessible by a short walk from a layby however, parking is limited and it can be a boggy walk through the woods.

Alternatively you can begin your walk at the Old Smiddy and head west along the main road before turning onto Pitmurchie Road. After about 200 metres, look for the signpost marking the Deeside Way.

-> Follow the trail past houses and as you descend a steep hill, you'll pass a small hut on your right. Continue through a stretch of cleared forest until you reach a wooden fence with a marker pointing to Dess Waterfall and you will see it just around the corner.
///spits.equipping.zealous

11. Craigievar Castle

Craigievar Castle is like something out of a fairytale and one of Scotland's more unique castles. Craigievar Castle is one of the most loved and well kept castles in Scotland and the exterior remains pretty much unchanged since it was built in 1626, retaining much of its original charm, with ornate turrets, corbelled towers, and beautifully preserved interiors featuring historic furniture and paintings. It is also unsurprisingly said to have inspired Walt Disney's iconic Cinderella Castle.

Craigievar Castle is owned by the National Trust for Scotland, therefore if you are a member you will have free entry and parking. An adult ticket is £17 with concession and family options available. It is also possible to enter the castle for a guided tour if you book a visit online.

-> Dogs are allowed in the grounds on a lead but not inside the castle. The estate has some accessible paths, but the castle itself has limited accessibility due to its historic nature. ///sobs.plates.motored

12. Castle Fraser

Castle Fraser is one of the largest tower houses in Scotland and the oldest parts of it date back to the 14th-15th century. Within the castle grounds there are some beautiful walks, including a 19th century walled garden, as well as a children's play area.

A tour of the castle takes around 45-60 minutes where you will be able to discover some of the many peculiarities that sit hidden around the castle.

The property is owned by the National Trust for Scotland, therefore if you are a member you will have free entry and parking. An adult ticket is £17 with concession and family options available. There is also a tearoom in the castle and toilet facilities, and the East Wing of the castle is available for self-catering holiday stays.

-> *Dogs on leads are welcome throughout the grounds. The castle offers some accessible facilities, including parking and toilets. Wi-Fi is available in certain areas. ///operation.perkily.rail*

12 Castle Fraser, Garden & Estate

11 Craigievar Castle

13. Crathes Castle

Crathes Castle, Garden and Estate, a beautiful place to visit on your NE250 road trip, taking you back to the 16th century. It was built in the 16th century by Alexander Burnett after Robert the Bruce granted him the land. The Burnett family continued to live in the castle for over 350 years.

Located just outside of Banchory in Aberdeenshire, Crathes Castle is only a short drive from Aberdeen city. There is a large car park that is shared with Go Ape and it costs £3 to park, or is free if you are a Natioanl Trust member. If you are a member you will also have the benefit of entering the castle for free. It is free to roam the castle grounds and take beautiful photos. An adult ticket to enter the castle is £17 with concession and family options available.

-> Dogs are permitted in the grounds on a lead but not inside the castle or walled garden. The estate provides accessible parking and paths. Wi-Fi is available in the café area. ///passport.stag.stormy

14. Drum Castle - Garden & Estate

Drum Castle Garden and Estate is one of Scotland's oldest tower houses. It lies on the outskirts of Banchory, not far from the city centre of Aberdeen.

Robert the Bruce granted William de Irwyn the castle and its grounds in 1323 and the castle remained in the Irvine clan until 1975. Later, a Jacobite mansion was added and in the Victorian era the lower halls were converted into a library. This is now home to over 4,000 books!

This is also a National Trust site so is free for members, or a £17 with concession for adults.

-> Dogs on leads are welcome in the grounds. The castle has accessible parking and some ground-floor access. Wi-Fi is available in the tearoom. ///pipeline.clincher.weeded

15 Dunnottar Castle

15. Dunnottar Castle

Perhaps one of Scotland's most picturesque castles, Dunnottar Castle sits proudly perched on the edge of a cliff, completely surrounded by the sea apart from the narrow entrance that bridges it to the mainland. Built in the 14th century and used until the 17th century, it was once lived in by the most powerful family in Scotland, the Keiths. As a castle that looks utterly , it is easy to see why it was in use for so long.

Tickets can be purchased online in advance or at the castle (they currently only take card payments). Prices for an adult are £13 and child £6. The tickets allow you entry into the castle grounds, however you can still get some cracking photos without a ticket from the nearby cliffs. It is also worthwhile visiting the nearby town of Stonehaven for an ice cream and a wander. This quaint harbour town has a beautiful beach and lots of cute cafes and shops to explore.

-> *Dogs allowed on leads throughout the site. Due to its cliff-top location, access involves steep steps and uneven paths, making it challenging for those with mobility issues. No Wi-Fi facilities on-site. ///emptied.beak.torched*

Where to Eat
in Braemar & Royal Deeside

Cafes

- **Café Noir Coffee House** - Stonehaven - Habourside cafe ///tricycle.freshen.array
- **The Bothy** - Braemar - Cosy vibes with a beautiful decking ///pill.stunt.noses
- **Tarmachan Cafe** - Crathie - Minimalist cafe with artisan food ///tripling.ended.others
- **Potarch Café** - Banchory - Beautiful interior ///matrons.interviewer.tactical
- **Birdhouse Cafe** - Banchory - Cute cafe with great cakes ///sparkle.occur.resurgent
- **Ride Coffee House** - Banchory - Quirky cafe with skate shop ///waltzed.wreck.gums
- **Scolty Cafe** - Banchory - A friendly local cafe ///reward.wimp.expensive
- **Highlanders Bakehouse** - Crathie - Rustic cafe vibes ///endearing.staining.scribble

Restaurants

- **Farquharsons Bar & Kitchen** - Braemar - Classic pub food ///jetting.duke.majoring
- **Clachan Grill** - Baillieston - Pub food with beer garden ///meaty.every.track
- **Kildrummy Inn** - Kildrummy - Luxurious & great food ///list.riding.dunk
- **The Alford Bistro** - Alford - Great for vegan options ///paintings.bliss.hippy
- **Borsalino** - Peterculter - Classic Italian food ///mercy.knees.hormones

Where to Stay
in Braemar & Royal Deeside

Hotels, B&Bs & Self-catering
- The Green Inn Rooms, Ballater - Traditional pub & hotel - ///grows.stiletto.glows
- Cambus o'May Hotel, Ballater - Victorian hunting lodge - ///inches.decently.roofer
- Aberdeen Arms Hotel, Tarves - Old fashioned pub & hotel - ///backswing.ages.speak
- The Ship Inn, Stonehaven - Cosy harbourside hotel - ///scorecard.gripes.spot
- Haughton Arms Hotel - Grand manor hotel - ///keep.brotherly.liability
- Cranford Guest House - Quaint guesthouse - ///keep.brotherly.liability
- Crathie Opportunity Holidays - Luxurious cottages - ///breeze.tools.vegans

Campsites
- Braemar Caravan Park & Camping Pods - ///pictured.evenings.recitals
- Ballater Caravan Park - ///colder.entry.headstone
- Tarland Camping & Caravanning Club Site - ///march.cabs.weeknight
- Silverbank Caravan & Motorhome Club Campsite - ///clutches.kingpin.improves
- Feughside Caravan Park - ///firming.blazers.reporting
- Stonehaven Caravan & Motorhome Club - ///hooks.nuance.interrupt

Roadtrip Essentials
in Braemar & Royal Deeside

Food Shops
- **Greens of Braemar** - ///acids.twirls.taskbar
- **Co-op Food - Ballater** - ///executive.grudge.hissing
- **Deeside Deli & Garden Shop** - ///clouds.rucksack.shaves
- **Co-op Food - Aboyne** - ///throwaway.swim.cyber
- **Tesco Superstore - Banchory** - ///stealthier.allowable.hero
- **Morrisons - Banchory** - ///firelight.amplifier.owns
- **Tesco Superstore - Stonehaven** - ///scouting.submitted.owned

Electric Vehicle Charging Points
- **Balnellan Road Car Park** - ///whistle.compiler.rocky
- **Ballater Golf Club** - ///initiated.removable.trickster
- **Station Square Car Park, Aboyne** - ///boardroom.ship.canny
- **Tesco Superstore, Banchory** - ///stealthier.allowable.hero
- **Kingswells Park and Ride, Aberdeen** - ///specifies.pumps.basher
- **Tesco Superstore, Aberdeen Woodend** - ///lovely.cope.update

Fuel Stations
- **Braemar Filling Station** - ///processor.beats.unites
- **Highland Fuel Station, Ballater** - ///pacifist.canine.guitar
- **Aboyne Service Station** - ///resides.ambitions.realm
- **Shell - Banchory** - ///upwards.snappy.radiates
- **Morrisons Petrol Station - Banchory** - ///feuds.everyone.soak
- **Tesco Petrol Station - Banchory** - ///paces.spits.berated
- **Fiddes Bridge Services - Stonehaven** - ///gown.flocking.loafing

Campervan Facilities
- **Toilets & Fresh Water, Balmoral Tourist Centre** - ///fine.gone.shallower
- **Fresh Water, Fuel station, Dunnoter Avenue** - ///pastime.overlaps.media
- **Serviced Laundry, Margaret St, Stonehaven** - ///behind.diver.corals
- **Water tap, Shorehead, Stonehaven** - ///rotations.squares.circle
- **Waste Disposal, Fresh Water & Toilet Block, Muir of Dinnet Visitor Centre** - ///dollar.scrapping.televise

7 Muir of Dinnet National Nature Reserve

SIGHTS

Lighthouse 16. Girdle Ness Lighthouse

Towns 17. Footdee
 23. Belmont Street
 24. Union Street

Beaches 18. Aberdeen Beach

Nature Spots 19. Duthie Park
 21. Union Terrace Garden
 30. Seaton Park

Castles & Historical Sights 20. Powis Gates
 27. Marischal College
 29. William Wallace Statue

Churches 22. Kirk of St Nicholas
 25. St Machar's Cathedral
 26. Greyfriars Church
 28. St Andrew's Cathedral

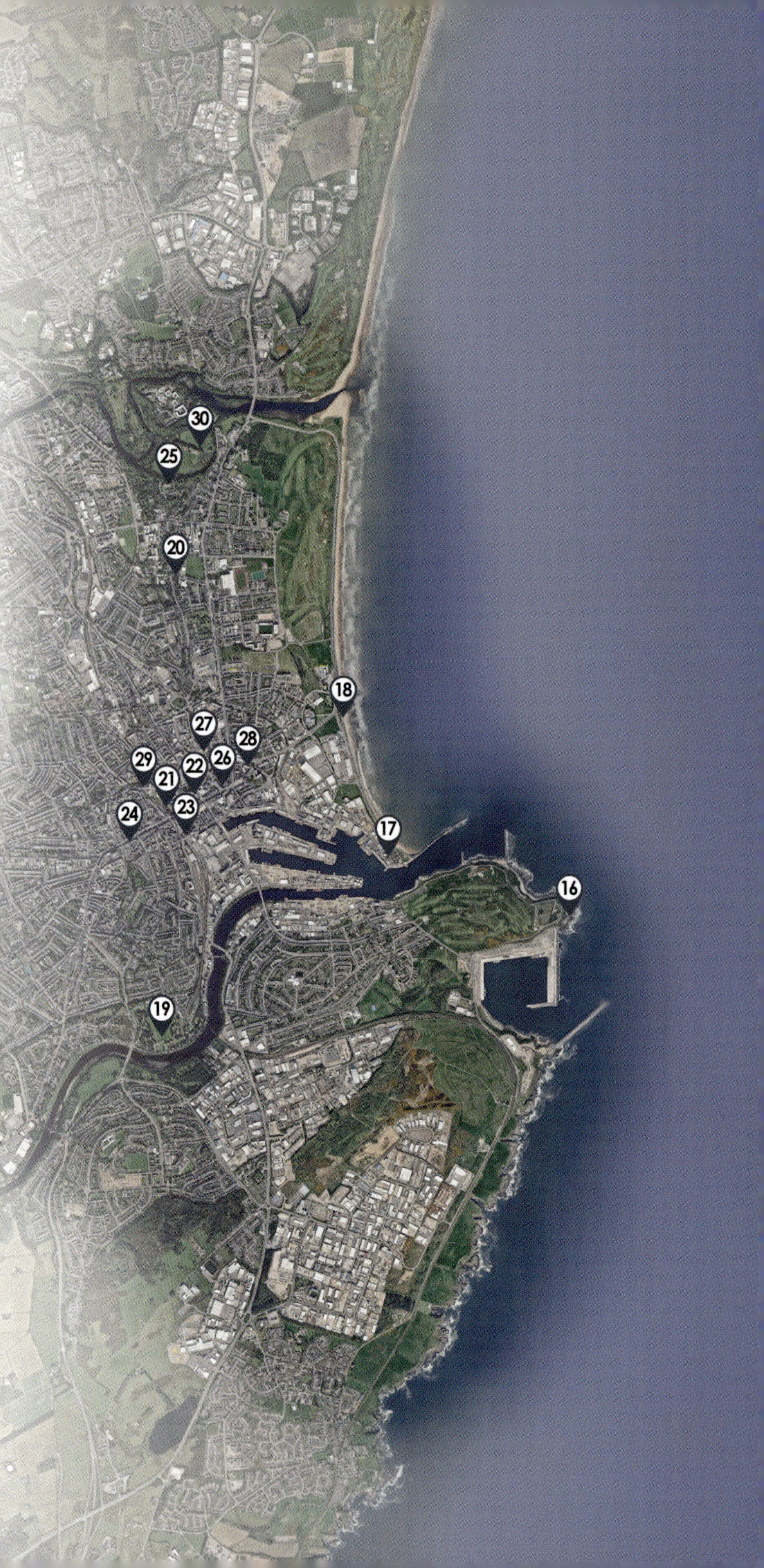

Aberdeen

Where the wild North Sea crashes into the Scottish mainland, Aberdeen rises in a glimmer of silver and stone. Known affectionately as the Granite City, Aberdeen is a place where nature, industry, and culture have collided over centuries to create one of Scotland's most distinctive cities. Built from locally quarried granite that sparkles in the sunlight and weathers beautifully in the rain, Aberdeen's handsome architecture tells a story of ambition, resilience, and reinvention.

Aberdeen has been a hub of life for thousands of years, with its two rivers, the Dee and the Don, providing natural harbours that nurtured early settlements. As time marched on, the city grew into one of Scotland's most important trading ports, exporting textiles, fish, and granite around the world. In the 20th century, Aberdeen's fortunes were transformed once again with the discovery of North Sea oil, earning it the nickname "Europe's Oil Capital" and bringing a new era of prosperity and innovation.

Despite its industrial prowess, Aberdeen has never lost its connection to nature. Stretching along its eastern edge lies a beautiful beach that could rival those found further around the coast, just minutes from the city centre. Further afield, the rolling landscapes of Aberdeenshire offer a true outdoor playground, from the fairytale castles of Royal Deeside to the towering mountains of the Cairngorms National Park.

Aberdeen is also a city of culture, home to one of Scotland's oldest universities, a vibrant arts scene, and a calendar full of festivals celebrating music, theatre, and innovation. Its maritime heritage runs deep too, a stroll through the city's old fishing quarter, Footdee, reveals a charming village frozen in time, while the bustling harbour continues to send ships and ferries out into the North Sea every day.

Today, Aberdeen is undergoing another exciting chapter, with renewed investment in tourism, sustainability, and the arts breathing fresh life into its granite heart. It's a city that proudly honours its past while confidently stepping into the future.

For visitors, Aberdeen offers the best of both worlds: the energy and excitement of a dynamic city, paired with immediate access to some of the most breathtaking natural landscapes in Scotland. Whether you come for the history, the prmenade walks along the beach, the food scene or the nightlife, a good time by all is sure to be had on a visit to Aberdeen.

16. Girdle Ness Lighthouse

Girdle Ness Lighthouse is an active lighthouse situated near Torry Battery on the Girdle Ness Peninsula. It has been open since 1833 and sits south of the entrance to the Aberdeen harbour and was built after the whaler Oscar was wrecked in 1813, killing all but two of the crew. It consists of a 37 metre white cylindrical tower, with its light positioned at an elevation of 56 metres above sea level, and was automated in 1991.

It is common to see dolphins in the area, particularly in the morning. Parking is available nearby.

-> *No access to the public to the lighthouse itself, however, there is plenty of parking nearby. ///loyal.whips.limp*

17. Footdee

Whilst you are in Aberdeen you must visit the small harbour village of Footdee, known as "Fittie" by locals. This charming historic fishing village is lined with quaint houses designed in the early 19th century to rehouse the city's fishing community, near Aberdeen Harbour. It sits tucked away at the end of the esplanade and if you weren't looking for it, it is unlikely you would find it.

The village features a unique layout of inward-facing cottages arranged around communal squares, providing shelter from the harsh North Sea winds. It is a lovely place for a walk around the narrow lanes, admiring the uniform granite cottages and the eclectic, brightly painted outhouses that reflect the residents' individuality.

-> *Parking is available along the esplanade and then you can walk to the village. ///comet.record.cheese*

18. Aberdeen Beach

Aberdeen Beach, stretching along the North Sea coast between the harbour and the River Don is a popular place to see swimmers and surfers at sea. Historically, it featured a bathing station in the early 20th century, reflecting its longstanding appeal as a seaside retreat. Today, the beach is renowned for its sands and a scenic promenade that extends from the historic fishing village of Footdee to the Don estuary.

This promenade is ideal for walking, jogging, and cycling, offering panoramic sea views and the chance to spot dolphins near the harbour entrance.

If you are feeling up to it, Scot Surf offer Surfing Lessons & Stand Up Paddle Boarding from their trailer on the esplanade. Alternatively, you may wish to explore the many cafes and ice cream shops that line the shore, or even pay a visit to the local amusement park for some of the exhilarating rides. There is plenty of parking along the esplanade.

> -> Toilets available along the southern end and plenty of parking. Dogs are welcome year-round. The promenade is accessible, and some nearby cafés offer Wi-Fi. This is a good spot to park and walk into town. ///update.souk.ruler

18. Aberdeen Beach

20. Powis Gates

19. Duthie Park

Duthie Park is a popular family and dog friendly park in Aberdeen's Ferryhill area which opened to the public in 1883 after being gifted to the city by Miss Duthie in 1880. This 44 acre park is filled with wonderfully restored Victorian features such as a bandstand, boating ponds and statues. There are also many children's play parks and picnic benches.

The David Welch Winter Gardens can be found in Duthie Park and is one of the most visited public indoor plant collections in Scotland and one of Europe's largest indoor gardens. The Park Café is situated within the park and offers a selection of snacks, ice cream, and light meals.

-> Dog-friendly park with accessible paths and facilities. Two main car parks: one accessible from Polmuir Road and another along Riverside Drive///effort.happen.whites

20. Powis Gates

The Powis Gates are a 19th century structure on the grounds of the University of Aberdeen's King's College campus, located in Old Aberdeen. These twin cylindrical towers were built between 1833 and 1834 and once served as a grand and ostentatious entrance to Powis House As you are walking through Old Aberdeen it is worth looking out for this historical landmark.

-> Located across from the King's College and nearby the University of Aberdeen. ///crop.held.energy

21. Union Terrace Gardens

This Victorian park in Aberdeen city centre offers a tranquil green space amidst the city's granite architecture. It opened to the public in 1879 and features sunken gardens, landscaped terraces and covers approximately two and a half acres. The walkways are wheelchair accessible and a recent refurbishment sees the park with a new play area, public toilets and restored Victorian features.

-> Located just above the Uion Square ///gather.agreed.elbow

22. Kirk of St Nicholas

The Kirk of St Nicholas, often referred to as the "Mither Kirk" of Aberdeen, is Aberdeen's oldest church, with origins tracing back to the 12th century. Located in the city centre, it has long been a central place of religious and civic life. The church features a remarkable blend of medieval and modern architecture, with its grand spire dominating the skyline. Entry to the Kirk is free where you can see the church's impressive interior featuring stained glass windows and a fascinating network of crypts, including a 19th-century burial vault.

-> As an active place of worship, dogs may not be permitted inside. The church has accessible entrances. /// spring.castle.idea

23. Belmont Street

Belmont Street is like the social hub of Aberdeen, located in the heart of the city. It is renowned for its lively atmosphere, featuring a variety of shops, cafes, and restaurants and it is here you will find some of the best restaurants, bars and cafes in the city. It runs perpendicular to Union Street in the centre of the city.

-> A bustling area with various cafés and shops, many of which are dog-friendly and offer Wi-Fi. ///salads.fired.deeper

24. Union Street

Union Street, also known as the granite mile, is a vibrant hub where you will find some great high street shopping in the city centre of Aberdeen, stretching approximately one mile from Castlegate to the west end. In addition to Union Street, shopping centres have opened up nearby so there is plenty of shopping to be done.

-> Aberdeen's main thoroughfare with diverse shops and eateries Generally dog-friendly on the street, however accessibility varies depending on the shops and cafes. ///lifted.digs.lifts

25. St Machar's Cathedral

St Machar's Cathedral is a Church of Scotland church located in Old Aberdeen in the north of the city, dating back to the 12th century. It hasn't had a bishop since 1609, therefore it is only a cathedral by name and more of a high kirk. It is free to enter the cathedral and lovely to have a look around the very impressive architecture.

-> Dogs are not typically allowed inside. The cathedral has accessible entrances, but Wi-Fi is not available.
///duck.month.dragon

26. Greyfriars Church

Greyfriars Church in Aberdeen is an often overlooked architectural gem located within the grand Marischal College complex. Greyfriars dates back to the mid 1500s and was originally part of a Franciscan friary, one of several monastic houses that once thrived in medieval Aberdeen.

While Greyfriars Church isn't generally open to the public, you can appreciate its history and craftsmanship from the outside, and it's a lovely spot for photography, especially in the soft light of early morning or late afternoon.

-> Dogs are not typically allowed inside. The cathedral has accessible entrances, but Wi-Fi is not available.
///shower.empire.rainy

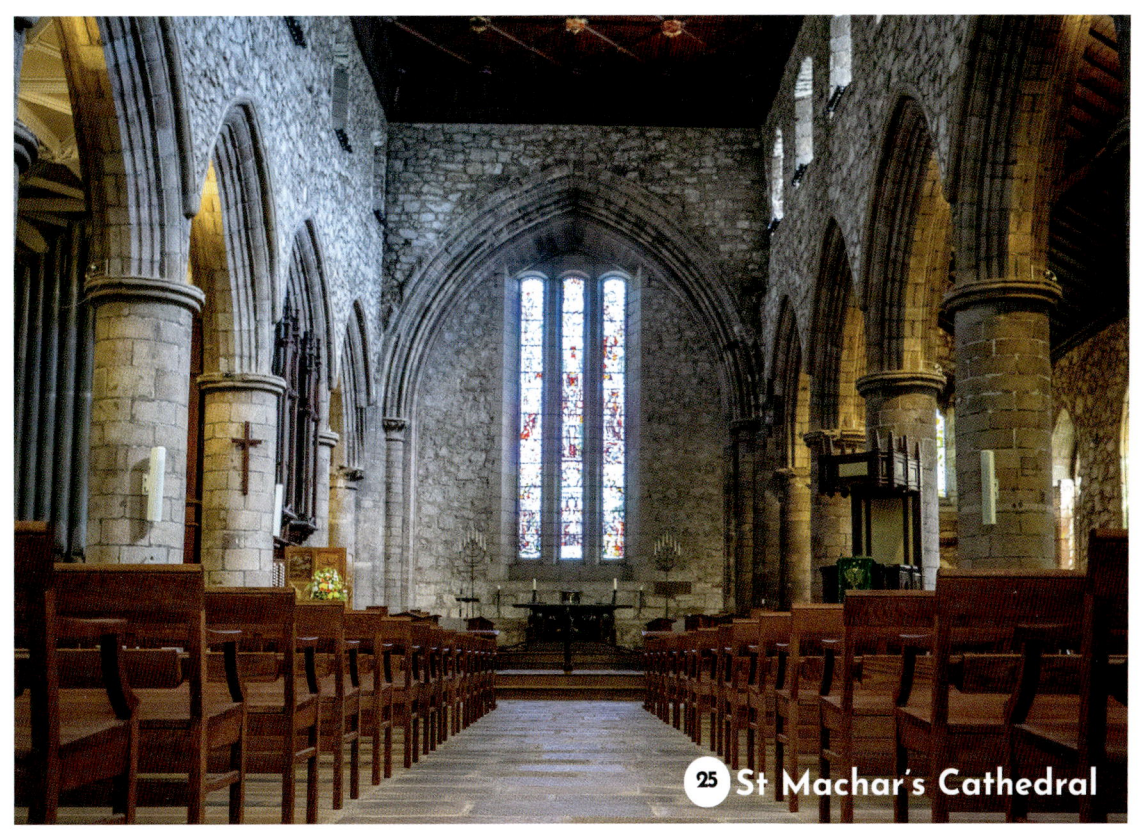

25 St Machar's Cathedral

27. Marischal College
Marischal College is one of the most eye pleasing buildings in the city of Aberdeen, located on Broad Street and renowned for its neo-Gothic architecture. The building was previously constructed for the University of Aberdeen, however, it is now used by the Aberdeen City Council. Construction on this building began in 1837 and it was recently renovated in 2011. While the building is not generally open for public tours, it is a beautiful building to admire during your visit to Aberdeen.

-> An iconic building housing Aberdeen City Council; public access is limited.   ///rots.transmitted.views

28. St Andrew's Cathedral
St Andrew's Cathedral is located on Kings Street in the heart of Aberdeen city centre. It is a beautiful building that stands out on the street. The church opened in 1817 as St Andrew's Chapel and was raised to cathedral status in 1914. This historical building is well known for being the church where the first bishop of the Episcopal Church in the USA, Samuel Seabury was ordained in 1784.

-> Dogs are generally not permitted inside. The cathedral offers accessible facilities, but Wi-Fi is not available.
   ///fries.nods.herb

29. William Wallace Statue
If you know Scotland, you will have heard of William Wallace. William Wallace is famous for his role in defeating the English army at Stirling Bridge and there are more than 20 statues of him across the country. This particular statue in Aberdeen was erected in 1888 and is positioned opposite the Union Terrace Gardens and His Majestys Theatre. It has text inscribed on each of its four sides reading well known phrases of the Scottish hero.

-> An outdoor monument accessible to all; dogs are welcome on leads. No Wi-Fi or additional facilities are present.
   ///hopes.secret.milky

30. Seaton Park
To the north of the city is Seaton Park, a beautiful place to swap the bustle of the city for the tranquility of Aberdeen's largest and most picturesque green space, encompassing 27 hectares along the River Don. There is a large garden area with beautiful plants, the perfect place for a picnic during the summer months. There is also a children's play area, public toilets and parking available.

-> A dog-friendly park with accessible paths and open spaces. Facilities are limited, and Wi-Fi is not available.
   ///jabs.length.hurt

Where to Eat
in Aberdeen

Cafes

- Cafe Noir Coffee House - Stonehaven - Habourside cafe   ///tricycle.freshen.array
- The Cult Of Coffee - Aberdeen - City centre coffee stop ///drip.legs.change
- The Long Dog Cafe - Aberdeen - Unique sweets and drinks ///images.tight.putty
- 210 Bistro - Aberdeen - Great views of the harbour ///pads.tigers.solved
- No.10 Bar and Restaurant - Aberdeen - Cosy bar vibes ///grass.sweep.upon
- Books and Beans - Aberdeen - Cute book shop & cafe ///pirate.kinks.table
- Morad's Beach Front Cafe - Aberdeen Promonade ///agents.cares.slap

Restaurants

- Cafe Andaluz - Aberdeen - Fine dining Italian ///crew.hurry.guard
- Maggie's Grill - Aberdeen - Bar and Grill ///fumes.zips.tribune
- Aperitivo Italian Restaurant - Aberdeen - Quaint Italian ///points.suffer.bubble
- Wild Boar - Aberdeen - Traditional Pub Grub ///escape.played.bridge
- Amarone - Aberdeen - Italian with beautiful interior ///expose.hood.limit

Where to Stay
in Aberdeen

Hotels, B&Bs & Self-catering
- Palm Court Hotel - A charming 4-star, city-centre hotel ///dirt.agreed.woof
- The Brig Inn Hotel - Family friendly in North Aberdeen ///souk.clubs.baked
- Ardoe House Hotel & Spa - Country manor house hotel ///void.truth.shaped
- Malmaison Hotel - Boutique & Stylish in city centre ///defeat.bets.deck
- Village Hotel - Aberdeen - Modern vibe with a pool ///trout.rewrites.enlighten
- Leonardo Hotel - Aberdeen - Stylish & city-centred ///paints.carbon.cook

Campsites
- Templars' Park Scout Campsite - Maryculter ///stolen.bandwagon.oaks
- Deeside Holiday Park - Maryculter ///parading.recently.panics
- Hillhead Caravan Park - Inverurie ///slams.mothering.crawled
- Seaview Caravan Park - Bridge of Don ///nasal.called.dispensed

17 Footdee

Roadtrip Essentials
in Aberdeen

Food Shops
- Tesco Superstore - **Stonehaven** - ///scouting.submitted.owned
- Lidl - **North Aberdeen** - ///brings.critic.expert
- Asda Superstore - **Aberdeen esplanade** - ///gazed.gained.maple
- Lidl - **South Aberdeen** - ///rises.pepper.tree
- Sainsbury's - **Northwest Aberdeen** - ///assure.rugs.dwell
- Aldi - **West Aberdeen** - ///media.author.mole

Electric Vehicle Charging Points
- Summer Street Car Park - ///adopt.casual.richer
- Aberdeen Railway Station - ///rocket.feared.garden
- Crombie Road, Aberdeen - ///hired.rushed.shared
- Northlink Ferries Terminal car park - ///spell.tube.stone
- Aberdeen Snowsports Centre ///vase.toward.rods
- Starbucks Intown Road - ///hiding.jazzy.stones

Fuel Stations
- Morrisons Petrol - Aberdeen - ///ladder.verbs.assist
- Shell - North Aberdeen - ///humans.rock.rivers
- BP - North Aberdeen - ///bother.spoke.chest
- Esso - Aberdeen - ///sits.action.traded
- Asda Petrol - Southwest Aberdeen - ///dozen.risky.smiles
- Sainsbury's Petrol - Southwest Aberdeen - ///locate.rated.person
- Tesco Petrol - West Aberdeen - ///retrieves.contracting.weary

Campervan Facilities
- Speedy Washes Launderette, Farmers Hall, Aberdeen - ///pint.fired.files
- LPG and Laundry Revolution, Shell, King St - ///humans.rock.rivers
- Gas bottles available, BP, King St - ///bother.spoke.chest
- LPG station, Kirkton Drive - ///passport.spreading.feed

Aberdeen Beach

16 Girdle Ness Lighthouse

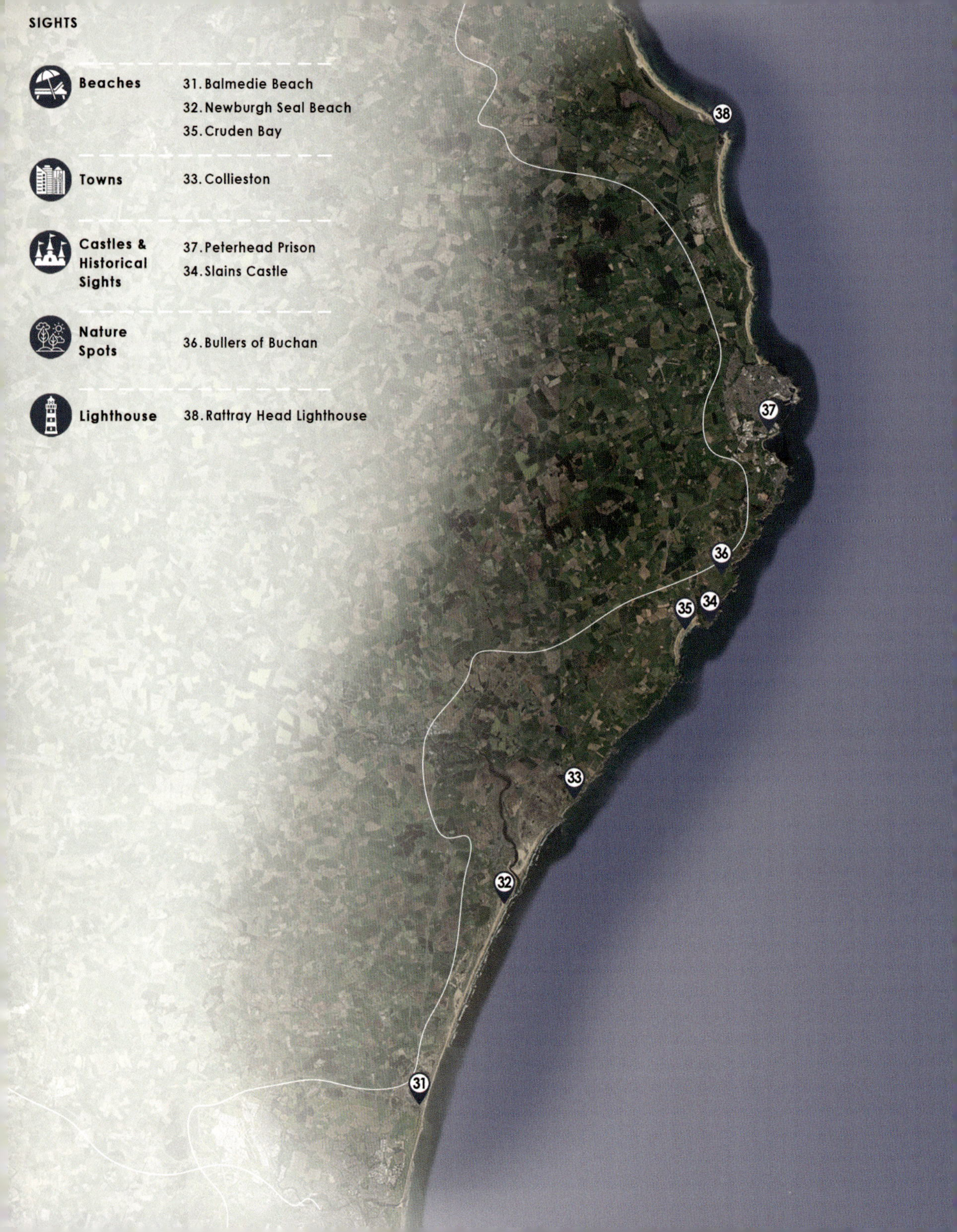

SIGHTS

 Beaches
- 31. Balmedie Beach
- 32. Newburgh Seal Beach
- 35. Cruden Bay

 Towns
- 33. Collieston

 Castles & Historical Sights
- 37. Peterhead Prison
- 34. Slains Castle

 Nature Spots
- 36. Bullers of Buchan

 Lighthouse
- 38. Rattray Head Lighthouse

The East Coast

Stretching north from the granite city of Aberdeen, the east coast of Aberdeenshire is a windswept and rugged landscape defined by dramatic cliffs, wide open beaches, and centuries of rich maritime history. This stretch of coastline offers a wilder, quieter escape from the more visited parts of Scotland, where the North Sea crashes against red sandstone cliffs, and tiny fishing villages huddle between bays and headlands.

From the vast, golden sands of Balmedie Beach to the seal-studded shores of Newburgh, nature takes centre stage here. Birdwatchers and wildlife lovers will find paradise in places like Collieston, a charming village backed by cliffs and known for its resident seabirds, or the Bullers of Buchan, a collapsed sea cave and natural amphitheatre of rock that teems with puffins, razorbills and guillemots during spring and summer.

No trip along this coastline would be complete without a visit to the brooding ruins of Slains Castle, perched precariously above the sea and long rumoured to have inspired the movie, "Dracula". Just south of it lies Cruden Bay, a sweeping arc of sand that has enchanted visitors and writers for generations.

Further north, the imposing Peterhead Prison Museum tells a darker, more recent story of Scotland's penal past, while the remote and haunting Rattray Head Lighthouse, standing sentinel off the coast in isolation, is a reminder of the wildness of this seaboard. The east coast of Aberdeenshire may be less travelled than other corners of the country, but it rewards those who venture here with solitude, beauty, and some of Scotland's most memorable coastal views.

31. Balmedie Beach

Balmedie Beach is located just north of Aberdeen and is a beautiful, peaceful country park and a vast stretch of golden sand backed by towering dunes. Its wide, flat shoreline is perfect for long walks or family days out on the beach. Wooden boardwalks wind through the dunes, leading to picnic spots, play areas, and toilets, making it accessible and family friendly.

The beach is dog friendly year round so it is a popular place with dog walkers. The Sand Bothy, a community run facility, provides a kiosk serving food and drink on weekends.

-> *Free parking is available at the North Car Park, which includes disabled spaces and toilet facilities.*
  ///arena.establish.harp

32. Newburgh Seal Beach

Newburgh Beach is one of the special spots in Scotland where you are guaranteed to see seals. It is a secluded spot just 15 minutes north of Aberdeen, on the coast of Newburgh Village.

Where the path meets the beach, you will see a small shipwreck off to the right. The River Ythan divides the banks where the seals have made their base on your left, however you will be able to see them basking on the shores or swimming up and down the water.

-> Dogs are allowed but should be kept on a leash to avoid disturbing the seals. The area has uneven terrain, which may pose challenges for those with mobility issues. There is a 2m height barrier to access the beach car park. If you are travelling in a larger vehicle you can park in the town or take public transport. ///texts.nasal.flopping

33. Collieston

Collieston is a small fishing village a short drive north of Newburgh. The breakwater that you can see was built in the 19th century, providing shelter from the harsh North Sea to the once bustling fishing harbour. After its construction, the small beach nearby was formed by the tides, and today offers the perfect spot for stretching your legs and admiring the stunning coastline. The nearby 'Smugglers Cone' shop serves delicious ice cream, drinks and snacks.

-> *This quaint coastal village welcomes dogs, especially along the shoreline. Facilities are limited, and the hilly terrain may be difficult for some visitors. ///draw.hurry.polka*

34. Slains Castle

The phenomenal ruins of New Slains Castle lie on the east coast, just outside of Cruden Bay. This ancient castle ruin is said to have been the inspiration for the one featured in the worldwide hit "Dracula". New Slains Castle was built in the 16th century, however, there has been significant reconstruction to the castle over the years.

The ruins are large with many beautiful views looking out to sea. It is possible to see that once there was a second floor in place, however, as nature has slowly reclaimed its place here, it is only possible to explore the ground floor of this once majestic castle.

-> There is a small, free car park at the side of the road and the walk to the castle is around 1km on a flat path. Dogs are welcome. The terrain is uneven and can be challenging. /// regular.hardly.procured

35. Cruden Bay

Cruden Bay is a small fishing village that sits on the edge of the Bay of Cruden, a gorgeous white sandy beach on the eastern coast of Scotland. The beach is 2.5km long and is accessed from a small wooden "Ladies Bridge" footbridge in the village.

This area is closely linked with the nearby Slains Castle due to its connections to the Erroll family. In addition to this, The Earl of Erroll was also involved in the construction of the nearby harbour, Port Erroll which remains in use today with good views along Cruden Bay.

-> The beach is dog-friendly year-round. Access points include steps and paths that may be steep. Public toilets are available in the nearby town. ///billiard.snowy.shut

35 Cruden Bay

36. Bullers of Buchan

A natural phenomenon that sits along the cliffs of the eastern coast of Aberdeenshire, the Bullers of Buchan is a collapsed sea cave that now consists of the 30m deep circular cliff edge, alive with the sound of birds. From this one spot alone, it is possible to see puffins, kittiwakes, guillemots, razorbills, shags, gulls, and even seals, and dolphins.

The walk to reach the cliff edge is flat and takes around 10 minutes. Watch your feet carefully around here as there is a 30m drop from a very thin grassy path. Just be prepared for the smell.. You can't have this many sea birds in one place without a noticable odour.

-> There is a small car park and a path leading down to the sea. Dogs are allowed but should be kept on leads due to steep drops. The path is uneven and not accessible. ///fewer.obstruct.diverting

37. Peterhead Prison

Peterhead Prison was one of Scotland's most notorious prisons, known for being a brutal prison that held some of Scotland's most violent criminals. It operated from 1888 to 2013 and has since opened as Peterhead Prison Museum.

You can take a tour of this former prison and learn the story of the Prison's history which saw the only time the SAS were used to end a domestic siege in Britain. If you are visiting during October, look out for their popular Halloween Tours.

-> Located in the centre of Peterhead. Only assistance dogs are permitted. The museum is wheelchair accessible, with lifts and ramps throughout.
 ///feasted.increment.internal

38. Rattray Head Lighthouse

This is one of those places that you visit not having any expectations and it just wows you. After driving down a rather bumpy off road track for around 1.5km, you will reach a small, muddy parking area.

Follow the grassy path through the gate and take the path that heads to the right. From here you will be immersed between sand dunes and walking through soft white sand. As you walk through you will see the lighthouse out at sea and an endless white sandy beach completely surrounding you. A true hidden gem on Scotland's east coast.

-> The surrounding beach area is dog-friendly. Access involves walking over dunes and uneven ground, which may be challenging for some. Parking is at the end of a rough road. ///splinters.buildings.shred

Where to Eat
on the East Coast

Cafes
- **The Chinwag Cafe** - Newmachar - Homemade bakes ///gossiping.flotation.however
- **Trellis Coffee Shop** - Newburgh - Garden-themed café ///hourglass.reforming.dustbin
- **Harbour Dunes** - Port Erroll - Hearty lunches ///gloom.defected.mandates
- **Cornkist - Ellon** - Welcoming with locally sourced meals ///incisions.hinders.signs
- **Dolphin Cafe** - Peterhead - Homemade treats & sea views ///encodes.totals.belonging
- **The Coffee Apothecary** - Udny & Ellon - Specialty coffee ///documents.takeover.records
- **SYMPOSIUM coffee house Lido** - Peterhead - Seaside views ///sizes.warblers.before
- **Nikimax Cafe - Peterhead** - Nearby the town centre ///flipper.grapevine.afflicted
- **Cafe Nineteen** - Peterhead - Laid-back meal or coffee break ///troubles.mixing.extra

Restaurants
- **The Dunes Restaurant & Bar** - Balmedie - Coastal views ///tooth.tune.hardback
- **BrewDog DogTap** - Ellon - A quirky bar with craft beer ///yesterday.lucky.matchbox
- **The Village Chipper** - Boddam - Town favourite chip shop ///printing.gather.foreheads
- **Clerkhill Fishbar** - Fresh seafood takeaway ///putty.buzzing.windpipe
- **Kilmarnock Arms Hotel** - Cruden Bay - Historic 19th-century inn ///city.petulant.kilt

33 Collieston

Where to Stay
on the East Coast

Hotels, B&Bs & Self-catering
- Aikenshill House B&B - Cute highland cows on site   ///sneezed.aliens.embellish ♿ 📶 🐾
- Buchan Braes Hotel - Stylish 4-star retreat   ///monkey.rags.sleeps ♿ 📶 🐾
- St. Olaf Golf Hotel - Golf course adjacent   ///drill.alas.steady ♿ 📶 🐾
- Seaview Hotel - Grand house with a sea view   ///asset.softest.dispenser ♿ 📶 🐾
- Waverley Hotel - Centrally located in Peterhead   ///vowed.refuse.grit ♿ 📶 🐾
- Wildflower Eco Lodges - Peaceful glamping pods   ///teams.inflates.else ♿ 📶 🐾
- Tahuna Bothies - Luxury glamping pods   ///prongs.elevate.hubcaps ♿ 📶 🐾

Campsites
- Seaview Caravan Park - Aberdeen   ///nasal.called.dispensed ♿ 📶 🐾
- Craighead Holiday Park - Peterhead   ///setting.shudders.struggle ♿ 📶 🐾
- Aden Caravan & Camping - Mintlaw   ///nagging.airtime.indicated ♿ 📶 🐾
- Peterhead Marina Bay Holiday Park   ///jolt.scornful.lied ♿ 📶 🐾

35 Cruden Bay

Roadtrip Essentials
on the East Coast

Food Shops
- Co-op Food - Balmedie ///severe.secret.brand
- Premier - Newburgh ///handrail.diary.twee
- Tesco Superstore - Ellon ///instructs.barrel.doghouse
- Paterson's - Cruden Bay ///croaking.provider.cakes
- ALDI - Peterhead ///commander.wins.siblings
- Morrisons - Peterhead ///outwards.talker.exams

Electric Vehicle Charging Points
- Balmedie Library - ///entertainer.reverses.months
- Ellon Park & Ride - ///reserves.fixated.fluctuate
- Brew Dog Mega Tap, Ellon - ///haircuts.shoppers.bother
- Cruden Bay Golf Club - ///beanbag.similar.downs
- Starbucks Coffee Peterhead - ///saunas.husbands.readjust
- West Pier Car Park, Peterhead - ///horn.asterisk.riddle

Fuel Stations
- Esso - Ellon ///resembles.sadly.forks
- Esso - Peterhead ///poets.cheering.funky
- Morrisons - Peterhead ///fuss.diplomas.spires
- Asda - Peterhead ///sprinting.dive.interests
- Kessock Service Station - Fraserburgh ///persuade.caravans.pounces

Campervan Facilities
- Waste Disposal, Fresh Water - Cruden Bay Harbour Aire ///familiar.pizzas.easygoing
- Waste Disposal, Fresh Water - Glenbuchty Stopover Aire ///proudest.curbed.runways
- Laundry and LPG station - Don Service Station Aberdeen ///caller.lands.mixed

32 Newburgh Seal Beach

SIGHTS

Beaches
- 39. Waters of Philorth Beach
- 43. Rosehearty Beach
- 44. Aberdour Beach
- 46. Cullykhan Beach
- 53. Cullen Bay
- 68. Findhorn Beach

Lighthouse
- 63. Covesea Lighthouse
- 40. Kinnaird Head Castle Lighthouse and Museum

Castles & Historical Sights
- 41. Pittulie Castle
- 42. Pitsligo Castle
- 49. Duff House
- 52. Findlater Castle
- 56. Craigmin Bridge
- 57. Gordon Castle Walled Garden & Café
- 60. Spynie Palace
- 64. Duffus Castle
- 69. Nelson's Tower
- 71. Brodie Castle and Estate

Towns
- 45. Pennan
- 48. Gardenstown
- 50. Portsoy
- 51. Sandend
- 55. Strathlene
- 62. Lossiemouth

Viewpoints
- 47. Crovie Village Viewpoint
- 54. Bow Fiddle Rock

Nature Spots
- 58. WDC Scottish Dolphin Centre
- 66. Roseisle Country Park
- 67. Findhorn Bay Local Nature

Churches
- 59. Elgin Cathedral
- 65. Pluscarden Abbey

Distilleries
- 61. Glen Moray Distillery
- 70. Benromach Distillery

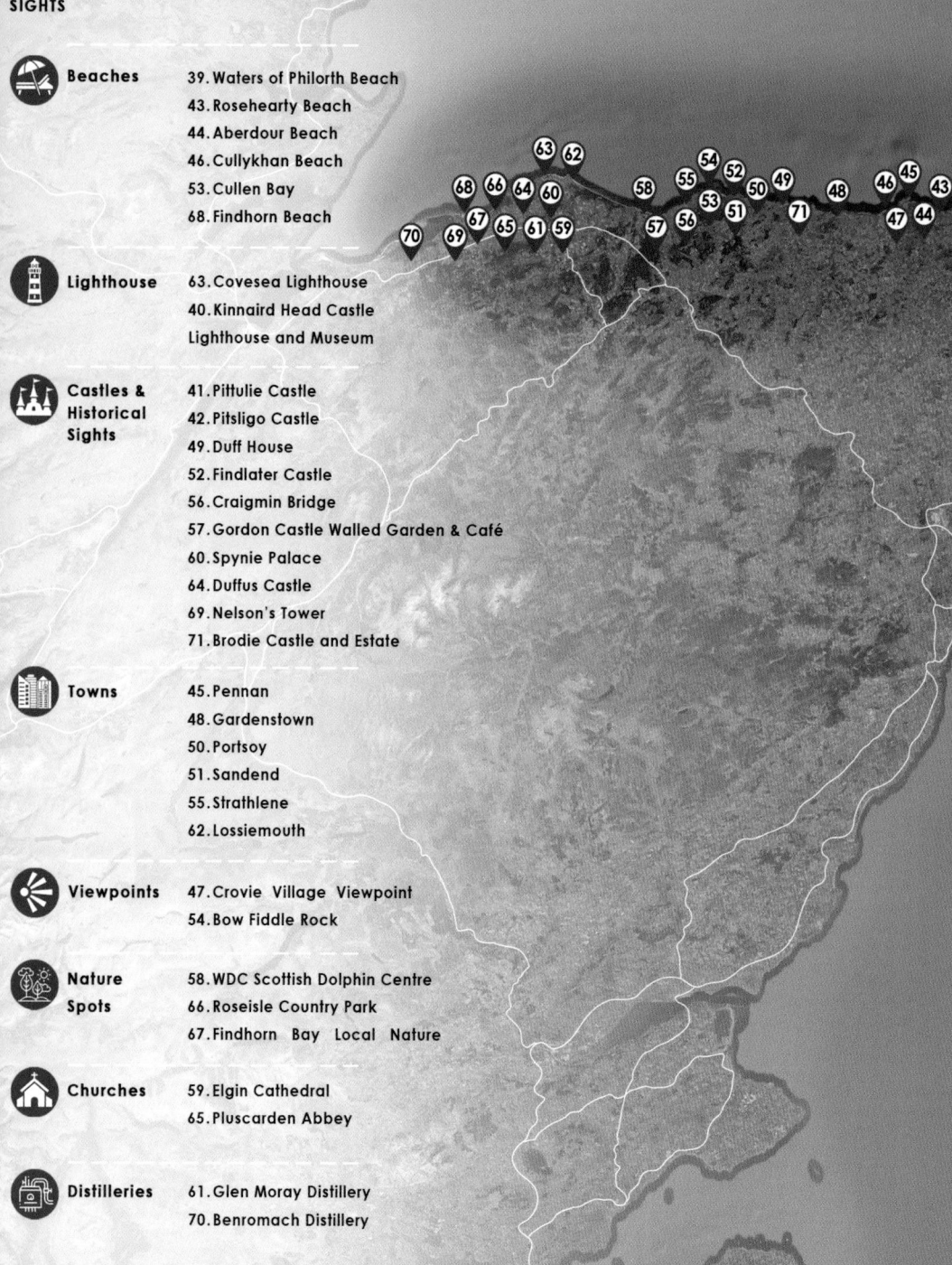

Moray Firth and Sunshine Coast

The Moray Firth and Sunshine Coast stretch is one of the most rewarding and diverse sections of the North East 250, offering a unique blend of golden beaches, clifftop castles, vibrant villages, and plenty of possibilities of seeing wildlife. Known as one of Scotland's sunniest regions, this coastline invites you to slow down and soak in its beauty, from the sweeping sands of Cullen Bay to the dramatic sea arch of Bow Fiddle Rock. Charming villages like Crovie and Gardenstown cling to the cliffs, seemingly untouched by time, while historic sems like Duff House and Elgin Cathedral offer a deep dive into Scotland's past.

This stretch is perfect for those who enjoy learning about Scottish history and being out in nature. There are plenty of peaceful coastal trails to wander along and look out for dolphins leaping in the firth, or maybe you want to sip whisky straight from the source at one of the region's famous distilleries. Whether you're exploring ancient ruins, walking barefoot on quiet beaches, or enjoying seafood in a harbour cafe, the Moray Firth delivers an unforgettable section of your road trip.

It's a side of Scotland that is entirely less travelled, but every bit as spectacular. If you're looking for calm, charm, and a touch of sunshine, this is where you'll find it.

54 Bow Fiddle Rock

39. Waters of Philorth Beach
The Waters of Philorth is a scenic and ecologically rich area located around two miles southeast of Fraserburgh. It encompasses a Local Nature Reserve and a sandy beach that stretches around 2km and is backed by impressive sand dunes which slope towards the water.

This beach is popular for both surfing and windsurfing and was a Marine Conservation Society recommended beach in 2006. This is a great place to look out for seals basking at Cairnbulg Point. Cairnbulg Castle is also not far from the beach.

-> *Follow the B9033 from Fraserburgh towards Inverallochy and look for the signed track to the Waters of Philorth. Free parking for around 40-50 cars. Access via sandy path with a rope-assist on the final dune section. Dog-friendly. Not wheelchair accessible. ///redefined.sobs.glove*

40. Kinnaird Head Castle Lighthouse and Museum
Kinnaird Head Castle Lighthouse and Museum is a unique site where Scottish history and maritime heritage come together. It was transformed into Scotland's first mainland lighthouse in 1787 by the Northern Lighthouse Board after originally being built as a 16th century castle for the Fraser family. The original tower remains an impressive feature of the lighthouse, with its light guiding ships safely along the treacherous northeast coast for centuries.

The site is home to the Museum of Scottish Lighthouses today, where you can explore the history and take an interesting tour of the lighthouse. The lighthouse remains very much how it was when its last crew members left it and a small, unmanned light nearby now fulfils the role of beacon.

-> *The museum can be found at the northern edge of the town. There is a large car park outside it. Assistance dogs are welcome.. The museum offers accessible facilities, including ramps and lifts. ///plotted.fortunate.baths*

41. Pittulie Castle
Pittulie Castle is a ruined 16th century tower house located near Rosehearty on the Aberdeenshire coast. Built by the Fraser family, the castle once stood as a stronghold overlooking the North Sea, strategically positioned for defence and trade. Though now in a state of ruin, with much of its structure collapsed, remnants of its walls and distinctive architectural features, such as gun loops and narrow windows, hint at its former grandeur. Today, the ruins stand in a cultivated field overlooking the sea, featuring a three storey square tower and remnants of a courtyard.

Access to the castle involves a level walk across farmland, being mindful of the crops. There are no on site facilities, however, parking is a 2km walk away in Rosehearty.

-> *Dogs are allowed but a leash is expected due to it being on private land. The terrain is uneven and may be challenging. ///surveyors.duplicity.tightest*

40 **Kinnaird Head Castle Lighthouse and Museum**

42. Pitsligo Castle

Pitsligo Castle is an impressive castle ruin with a rich history. It was built in the 15th century by the Forbes family and later expanded into an elegant residence, featuring a grand courtyard and intricate architectural details. It played a significant role during the Jacobite uprisings, with its owner, Lord Pitsligo, supporting Bonnie Prince Charlie in the 1745 rebellion.

After the Jacobite defeat, the castle was abandoned and fell into ruin, though its weathered walls and surviving structures still give us an idea of its former grandeur. Today Pitsligo Castle stands as a ruin overlooking the town of Rosehearty.

> -> Access to the castle involves a level walk across farmland, being mindful of the crops. There are no on-site facilities, however parking is a 1km walk away in Rosehearty. ///surveyors.duplicity.tightest

43. Rosehearty Beach

Rosehearty Beach sits on Scotland's northeast coast near Fraserburgh and is a sandy crescent shaped shoreline extending east from the village harbour, offering scenic views of the Moray Firth and nearby rocky outcrops such as Long Craig and Hungry Hoy.

The village of Rosehearty was established in the 14th century by Danish fishermen and evolved into a significant fishing port by the 19th century, with its harbour accommodating numerous fishing vessels during the herring season.

Rosehearty also features a 9 hole golf course and a Heritage Centre.

> -> The Rosehearty Community Boat Club offers £10 overnight parking on the seafront and nearby a large childrens play area. Public toilets are conveniently located adjacent to the beach. ///meal.dips.spruced

43 Rosehearty Beach

44. Aberdour Beach
Aberdour Beach is a secluded, crescent shaped beach featuring a mix of golden sand and smooth pebbles, and surrounded by rolling dunes. The rugged, dramatic, natural beauty of Aberdour Beach overlooks magnificent limestone caves nearby some great walking trails.

-> Follow the single track road down towards the beach where you will find a large car park sitting on the edge of the beach as well as picnic areas and toilet facilities. ///song.deferring.frozen

45. Pennan
Pennan is a charming and resilient coastal village, made up of a single row of whitewashed cottages that are nestled at the base of steep cliffs, facing the North Sea. This tiny village gained fame as the filming location for Local Hero (1983) and Whisky Galore (2016), drawing visitors from around the world. One of its most iconic landmarks is the famous red telephone box which has since been granted listed building status. This is a must see for fans of the cult classic Local Hero, which tells the story of an oil company attempting to buy a remote Aberdeenshire village. Pennan can also be a hotspot for wildlife spotting. Coastal Cuppie is a great coffee shack overlooking the harbour.

->The village is dog-friendly, with narrow streets leading to the harbour. Accessibility is limited due to steep paths, and facilities are minimal. ///homelands.sticky.inefficient

46. Cullykhan Beach
Cullykhan Beach is a small crescent shaped beach which is surrounded by cliffs and golden sands. There is plenty of parking and an accessible board walk leading down to the beach which is sheltered by rocky headlands. To the left of the beach is a sea level view of Pennan and by climbing up the hill to Fort Fiddes you will get a great birds eye view of the town and the site of an old Pictish Fort. This is an ancient defensive site that has seen occupation since prehistoric times.

->Dogs are allowed. The path to the beach is steep and uneven, posing challenges for accessibility. No facilities or Wi-Fi are available. ///sues.survived.flinches

47. Crovie Village Viewpoint & Car Park
Crovie is a fascinating place to visit on the NE250, that is quite unlike any other spot you will visit. This quaint coastal village consists of a single row of houses that sits tightly between the steep cliffs and the North Sea and has no shops, no phone signal and no roads. There is no room for cars along the narrow pathways so the locals have to transport their shopping by wheelbarrow from a car park at the top of the cliff.

Once a thriving fishing community, Crovie has retained its historic character, with many of its cottages now used as holiday retreats. The village offers stunning sea views, a sense of isolation, and a true escape from modern life. There is a viewpoint carpark with a beautiful view looking over Crovie from the top of the cliff with the option to walk to Gardenstown.

->Dogs are welcome. The village has steep and narrow pathways, making accessibility difficult.
  Car park located at ///fairly.munch.explorer

47 Crovie Village Viewpoint

48. Gardenstown

Gardenstown is a picturesque, hidden coastal village renowned for its tiered houses clinging to steep cliffs and winding lanes, offering stunning views of Gamrie Bay. This sheltered bay is a popular spot for wildlife sightings such as seabirds, dolphins, and seals. Gardenstown is a lovely place to explore and walk around, enjoying the local coffee shops and art galleries.

Its one of the best spots to visit on your NE250 road trip.

-> *A dog-friendly village with narrow, sloping streets. Accessibility may be challenging due to the terrain.
///forms.pollution.upstarts*

49. Duff House

Built in 1740 by renowned architect William Adam, Duff House is a magnificent mansion that should not be missed. Now housing a permanent collection of art from the National Galleries of Scotland, it has served many roles throughout its history, including a hotel and even a prisoner of war camp.

Duff House is managed today by Historic Environment Scotland and tickets are available to buy and explore the castle. It is cheaper to buy tickets online, adult £10 and child £6. The building itself is stunning and well worth getting some photos of the outside and there is also a children's play area outside.

-> *There is a main car park and accessible parking beside the house. Assistance dogs are welcome, not visitors dogs. The house offers accessible facilities, including lifts and ramps. ///webcams.pokes.lilac*

49 Duff House

50. Portsoy

Portsoy is a charming village known for its picturesque 17th century harbour which was more recently used as a Peaky Blinders filming location. The village of Portsoy is famous for its local jewellery and unique marble, which has been used in grand mansions and castles worldwide, including the Palace of Versailles.

You may also want to join the queue for some Portsoy ice-cream which serves up a selection of great flavours. This homemade ice cream is award winning and absolutely delicious artisan ice cream.

-> The village and harbour area are dog-friendly. Some paths may be uneven, affecting accessibility. Parking is generally plentiful around the town. ///televise.bitters.progress

51. Sandend

Sandend is one of the oldest fishing communities in Aberdeenshire dating back to the 1600's. This picturesque coastal village is known particularly for its rich fishing heritage. Nestled between Cullen and Portsoy, this small village offers stunning views of the Moray Firth and is a popular spot for surfers who will travel from across the country to experience the crashing waves at Sandend Beach. Sandend is also home to one of Scotland's oldest whisky distilleries, **Glenglassaugh** which also adds to its appeal, the best way to heat up after a surf!

-> The beach is dog-friendly. Access is relatively easy ///torn.airstrip.chariots

51 Sandend

52. Findlater Castle

Findlater Castle is an impressive castle ruin which is perched dramatically on a cliff overlooking the Moray Firth, dating back to the 13th century. The castle was once a stronghold of the Ogilvy and Sinclair families, strategically positioned for defence against seaborne attacks. Its name, derived from the Norse "Fyn-laiter," meaning "white cliff," which reflects its breathtaking coastal setting. In 1562, Findlater Castle was besieged by Mary Queen of Scots' forces. At the time, the castle was owned by John Gordon, who had rebelled against Mary.

You can still see remnants of its walls and stairways, blending into the rugged landscape despite the castle being in ruin. It is a fascinating place to visit, when you arrive at the car park prepare to walk 10 minutes on a grassy path towards the castle. You can either view the castle from the cliff or walk closer to it, however, the paths are very narrow and slippery so extreme care must be taken. It is also worth noting that this is a castle ruin and it may not be in a stable condition to step inside. **Be extremely careful.**

-> Accessible via a coastal path; dogs are allowed. The path is uneven and may be challenging for those with mobility issues.
///employers.editor.chest

53. Cullen Bay

One of the best-hidden gems of the North East of Scotland, the small town of Cullen, seemingly lost in time with enchanting rows of colourful terraced houses, sits overlooking the golden sandy beach and sea. It is easily one of our favourite beaches on the NE250.

The village is divided into two parts: the historic Seatown, with its traditional fishing cottages, and the newer upper town where you will find small shops, cafes and restaurants. The Cullen Bay Hotel is renowned for serving the traditional Scottish dish, Cullen Skink, a thick Scottish soup made of smoked haddock, potatoes and onions that originates here.

Beside the beach you will find two large car parks, one of which has a height barrier. Cullen Beach Burger Bar serves as a takeaway outlet beside the beach serving up a delicious menu including burgers, crepes, hot drinks and ice cream.

For the best view of Cullen, park up in the town centre and take the (slightly steep) walk to the top of Castle Hill. From here you can admire the view over the town, as well as the sweeping sands of the bay that stretch right along its front.

You will also notice the remains of the old towering Cullen Viaduct that spans the nearby river. This line was built in 1884 and once carried the Moray coastline around the Earl of Seafield's private estate to keep it away from the Earl's main residence.

Cullen Motorhome Stopover offers overnight parking on the seafront, which can be booked online and varies in price depending on the season.

-> Access to the seaside is easy with a large car park and flat promenade. The beach can be access by stone steps. It is dog-friendly all year round. The town itself my not be accessible due to how steep its streets are. ///banana.committee.irritated

54. Bow Fiddle Rock

Bow Fiddle Rock is a unique rock feature just off the coast of Portknockie. It is named the Bow Fiddle Rock as it looks like the tip of a fiddle bow. This natural sea arch was created by the pressure of the waves and wind coming in from the North Sea.

The towering rock is a haven for seabirds, including gulls and puffins, making it a popular spot for birdwatchers and photographers. Sunrise is a particularly good time to view the Bow Fiddle Rock when the light casts a golden glow on the rugged surface. Its unique shape and breathtaking surroundings make it a true marvel of Scottish geology and you can either view it from the top or walk down to the beach to enjoy the view.

-> There is a small amount of parking along the coast road or street parking is available in Portknockie. ///models.officer.presented

55. Strathlene

Strathlene is a peaceful coastal area on the northern coast of Moray. With stunning sea views and a sandy shoreline, it's a popular spot for those seeking a quiet seaside retreat. The area was once home to a thriving fishing community, and remnants of this past can still be seen in the nearby harbour and historic buildings. Strathlene is also a great place for spotting dolphins and seabirds. Strathlene Holiday Park overlooks the beach here as well as Strathlene Golf Club which is one of the oldest golf clubs in Scotland.

-> This coastal area welcomes dogs and offers scenic views. Facilities are limited, with no Wi-Fi, and the terrain may present challenges for visitors with mobility impairments. ///coats.bumping.gymnasium

54 Bow Fiddle Rock

56. Craigmin Bridge

Craigmin Bridge can be found hidden within the woodland near Buckie and is an impressive multi arched structure that showcases incredible 18th century engineering. Built with a unique double tiered design, the bridge spans a deep gorge, creating a impressive and almost mystical appearance, as it blends seamlessly with the surrounding trees and moss covered rocks.

Craigmin Bridge is believed to have been constructed in the 1770s and once served as an important crossing over the Burn of Buckie. It is a beautiful place for a walk through the woodlands.

-> *Dog-friendly, but the path through woodland may be uneven and challenging for accessibility. ///crazy.workloads.parading*

58. WDC Scottish Dolphin Centre

Located at Spey Bay, this centre offers a unique opportunity to observe Scotland's bottlenose dolphins in their natural habitat. Run by Whale and Dolphin Conservation (WDC), the centre is dedicated to protecting marine wildlife and educating visitors about conservation efforts.

It is free to enter and features interactive exhibits, wildlife walks, and a café with stunning views over the Moray Firth. As well as dolphins, you might spot ospreys, seals, and otters along the Spey River. You can also learn about Spey Bay's fishing heritage during a tour of the historic Tugnet Icehouse. It is worth noting that the WDC Scottish Dolphin Centre is open Wednesday - Sunday.

-> *Dogs are allowed on leads in outdoor areas but not inside the visitor centre. The site is wheelchair accessible and has Wi-Fi in the main building. ///reefs.easy.caring*

57. Gordon Castle Walled Garden & Café

One of Scotland's largest and most impressive walled gardens is Gordon Castle Walled Garden & Cafe. The beautiful walled gardens are open to the public all year round, however the castle is not open to the public. Originally built in the 18th century, the beautifully restored garden spans over eight acres and is bursting with vibrant flowers and featuring over 200 wall trained fruit trees, including the historic Gordon Castle plum.

Carefully maintained pathways have been built in to allow visitors to explore the gardens. The onsite cafe serves homemade dishes using ingredients grown within the garden, providing a true farm-to-table experience. Gordon Castle Highland Games and Country Fair continue today and tickets can be purchased on their website.

-> *Dogs are welcome in the outdoor garden and seating area but not inside the café. The garden has good accessibility with level pathways. Wi-Fi is likely available in the café.*
  ///powers.forgotten.imprinted

59. Elgin Cathedral

Elgin Cathedral, often referred to as the "Lantern of the North," is one of Scotland's most breathtaking medieval Gothic Cathedral ruins managed by Historic Environment Scotland. Dating back to the 13th century, this once grand cathedral was a symbol of the church's power and influence in Moray and was the main church for the bishops of Moray. In the 14th century, Elgin Cathedral was partially destroyed and later fell into ruin. Two towers with very intricate stonework and the remnants of stunning stained glass windows still stand today. If you are looking to experience some panoramic views over Elgin, you can climb the towers or alternatively, you can choose to explore the grounds, which include ancient tombstones and carved sculptures.

Elgin Cathedral is managed today by Historic Environment Scotland and tickets are available to buy and explore the castle. It is cheaper to buy tickets online, adult £10 and child £6.

-> *Dogs are allowed in the grounds but not inside the cathedral ruins. The site has some accessible pathways, though uneven surfaces may present challenges. ///bless.runs.always*

60. Spynie Palace
Spynie Palace served as the fortified residence of the Bishops of Moray for approximately 500 years. Established in the late 12th century, the palace was strategically positioned near Spynie Loch, a sea loch that provided safe anchorage for fishing boats and merchant vessels. Although the loch and the adjacent medieval settlement have since vanished, the palace remains the largest surviving medieval bishop's house in Scotland.

Spynie Palace is a great place to explore impressive ruins, including David's Tower, a six storey structure built in the 15th century, which stands as the largest by volume of all medieval Scottish towers and offers panoramic views of the surrounding countryside. Parking is available on site.

Spynie Palace is managed today by Historic Environment Scotland and tickets are available to buy and explore the castle. It is cheaper to buy tickets online, adult £7.50 and child £4.50.

-> Dogs are welcome in the grounds on a lead. Accessibility is limited due to uneven paths and historic ruins. No Wi-Fi on-site. There is onsite parking suitable for motorhomes just a short walk from the site. ///scaffold.standing.attends

61. Glen Moray Distillery
Dating back to the late 19th century, Glen Moray Distillery is located on the banks of the River Lossie in Elgin and has been producing single malt whisky since 1897. Known for its approachable, smooth character, Glen Moray offers a range of whiskies, from classic Speyside styles to expressions matured in sherry, port, and chardonnay casks. Glen Moray Distillery offer guided tours to learn about the distilling process, explore the traditional warehouses, and enjoy a tasting of their award winning drams. The distillery has a welcoming cafe and shop, perfect for picking up a bottle to take home.

-> The site is accessible, and Wi-Fi is available in the main building. ///gates.move.humble

62. Lossiemouth
Lossiemouth, affectionately known as the "Jewel of the North," is a historic seaside town with two expansive sandy beaches and a bustling marina. Lossiemouth was originally established as the port for Elgin in the 15th century and it has since evolved into a significant fishing hub.

It is a great town for a walk around, visiting the variety of local shops and eateries and plenty of parking is available around the beach. Lossiemouth offers overnight parking options for self-contained campervans for a small donation.

-> The town is dog-friendly, with beaches welcoming dogs year-round. Accessibility varies by location, and Wi-Fi is available in local cafes and public spaces. ///unclaimed.fronted.juniors

63. Covesea Lighthouse & Royal Navy and Royal Air Force Heritage Centre

Standing proudly on the cliffs west of Lossiemouth, Covesea Lighthouse is an iconic landmark offering sweeping views over the Moray Firth. This striking white tower was built in 1846 and once guided ships safely along the coast. Guided tours are ran here today allowing visitors to climb to the top, enjoying panoramic views and learning about the lighthouse's history. The nearby Royal Navy and Royal Air Force Heritage Centre tells the story of Moray's long aviation history, with fascinating exhibits on the nearby RAF bases and their vital role during wartime.

-> By car, turn off the B9040 towards Silver Sands Holiday Park. Just before entering the park, take a sharp left onto the single-track road leading to the lighthouse. There is a car park at the lower level near the Heritage Centre, from where it's a short 5-10 minute uphill walk to the Lighthouse. Vehicle access can be arranged for those requiring mobility assistance if this is mentioned when booking. ///stammer.thunder.cabbies

64. Duffus Castle

Duffus Castle was originally constructed as a timber motte-and-bailey in the 12th century before later being rebuilt in stone around 1305. The castle served as a fortress residence for over 500 years until its abandonment in 1705. Duffus Castle is an interesting place to explore the impressive ruins, including the partially collapsed tower that has slid down the motte, offering a vivid illustration of the site's historical evolution.

Duffus Castle is maintained by Historric Environment Scotland and is free to visit and open year-round. Parking is available approximately 15 metres from the entrance and if you are feeling peckish, Kula Coffee Hut operates from the car park.

-> Dogs are allowed on leads. The terrain is uneven, which may present accessibility challenges. No on-site Wi-Fi. Access to the castle itself is shut off to allow for regeneration of the grass surrounding it. ///poet.timer.withdraw

65. Pluscarden Abbey

Pluscarden Abbey is a peaceful, working Benedictine monastery nestled in a tranquil glen near Elgin. Founded in the 13th century, it remains the only medieval monastery in the UK still inhabited by monks and used for its original purpose. Visitors are welcome to explore the beautifully restored abbey church, admire the Gothic architecture, and enjoy the quiet atmosphere of its grounds.

The monks follow a traditional way of life, offering daily services sung in Gregorian chant, which visitors can quietly attend. Pluscarden is a place of quiet reflection and spiritual retreat, with no admission fee. While dogs are not allowed inside the abbey, they are welcome on leads in the surrounding grounds.

-> Dogs are not allowed inside the abbey. The grounds are accessible and motorhome suitable parking is available nearby. ///plod.coast.attends

64 Duffus Castle

66. Roseisle Country Park

A beautiful coastal escape on Forres on the Moray Firth known for its expansive sandy beach, towering pine forest, and network of walking and cycling trails. The park is owned by Forestry Land Scotland and offers plenty of picnic spots, BBQ facilities, and a play area. You might want to look out for seals offshore or red squirrels in the trees whilst you are here. There's ample paid parking and toilets onsite, and the paths are generally accessible for wheelchairs and buggies.

-> A dog-friendly woodland park with accessible trails. Small car park amongst the trees with picnic benches. ///frail.angers.relay

67. Findhorn Bay Local Nature Reserve

Findhorn Bay Local Nature Reserve is a peaceful tidal basin on Scotland's Moray coast, well known for its rich biodiversity and scenic beauty. This is a haven for birdwatchers who might catch a glimpse of migratory wildfowl and waders, including pink-footed geese and oystercatchers from the bird hide. Located only a short walk away from the idyllic village of Findhorn which offers a variety of coffee shops and restaurants.

-> Small car park by the side of the road. The region is dog-friendly and the bird hide is accessible. ///transcribes.presenter.rekindle

68. Findhorn Beach

Findhorn is a lovely little fishing village in Moray, located at the northern edge of the NE250 road trip, where the River Findhorn meets the Moray Firth. Overlooking the entrance to the Moray Firth, the lengthy beach of pebbles, golden sands and clear water is lined with quaint and colourful beach huts.

The town itself is small with plenty of delicious places to eat. There is parking in the town and by the beach as well as Findhorn Beach West Motorhome Stopover which is available to book online for £17/night, a short walk from the seafront. Accessible parking is also provided to the beach with an accessible boardwalk to the beach. Keep an eye out for seals at the north end of the beach.

The Watershed Sauna allows you to work up a sweat in a converted horse box before dipping in the sea and can be found on the beach hosting a variety of sessions and experiences.

Not far from the beach, you will be able to find the fascinating Heritage Centre, situated in the old Findhorn Ice House. The Icehouse is a fascinating exhibition of the fishing industry that was onced hosted in Findhorn. It consists of multiple underground arched chambers, built over 150 years ago and used to store ice for packing salmon to travel to London. The vast chambers are now used to display all aspects of the net salmon fishing industry in the Moray Firth.

-> Dogs are welcome on the beach, and accessibility is reasonable with designated pathways. Wi-Fi is available in nearby cafés. Toilets available just off the beach track. ///basically.cooking.order

69. Nelson's Tower

Standing high on Cluny Hill above Forres, Nelson's Tower is a unique monument dedicated to Admiral Lord Nelson to commemorate his naval victories. This impressive 21 metre high structure was built in 1806 in an octagonal shape and has four levels including the ground floor and rooftop.

Parking is available at Grant Park and it is a short but steep walk up taking around 15 minutes through the forest. There is the option to extend your walk on one of the many trails around the area.

-> *Dogs may be allowed in outdoor areas, but the steep climb and steps make accessibility challenging.*
///flocking.hurls.jumps

70. Benromach Distillery

Benromach Distillery is a small, traditional Speyside whisky distillery located on the outskirts of Forres. Established in 1898 and restored by Gordon & MacPhail in 1998, it's known for crafting single malt whisky by hand, using time honoured methods and natural ingredients. Benromach produces a distinctive style of Speyside whisky with a subtle hint of smoke, matured in first-fill casks to enhance its character. Benromach Distillery offer guided tours of the distillery to allow visitors to explore the traditional dunnage warehouses, and sample a range of whiskies in the welcoming tasting room.

-> *Dogs are not allowed inside. The visitor centre is accessible, and Wi-Fi is available. There is a large car park, suitable for small vehicles.* ///secondly.blanking.perfumes

71. Brodie Castle and Estate

Brodie Castle is located near Forres in Moray and is a 16th century Z-plan tower house that served as the ancestral home of the Brodie clan for over 400 years. The Brodie family's association with the area dates back to the 12th century. The castle was partially burned in 1645 and underwent significant remodeling in the 19th century.

Brodie Castle is open to visitors today to explore the castle's impressive interiors, which house fine antiques, intricate plaster ceilings, and an impressive art collection. The estate is famous for its magnificent gardens, especially in spring when over 100 varieties of daffodils burst into bloom.

The property is owned by the National Trust for Scotland, therefore if you are a member you will have free entry and parking. An adult ticket is £16 with concession and family options available. It is also possible to enter the castle for a guided tour if you book a visit online.

There is a visitor centre, gift shop, and cafe as well as plenty of onsite parking.

->*Dogs are welcome in the grounds but not inside the castle. The castle has good accessibility, and Wi-Fi is available in the visitor centre. There is a large car park with plenty of room for motorhomes.* ///bookings.pegs.masts

71 Brodie Castle and Estate

Where to Eat
on the Moray Firth and Sunshine Coast

Cafes
- Coastal Cuppie - Pennan - A cute coffee stand ///inhabited.migrants.standards
- Eli's Crafts, Cakes & Coffee - Banff - Great cakes ///sometime.land.intruding
- Kula Coffee Hut - Duffus Castle - Cute outdoor trailer ///conveying.reminder.dose
- Home Bakery - Macduff - Cute bakery ///showcases.scrub.fiction
- Cherry Tree Cafe & Bistro - Banff - Small and cute cafe ///affirming.cherry.uttering
- Coffee At The Kings - Cullen - Great views of the viaduct ///swatting.jams.tasteful
- Rockpool Cafe - Cullen - Town centre cafe ///scooped.strongly.stockpile
- Gulay's Patisserie - Cosy cafe with a wide range of food ///electrode.scorching.surreal
- The Bakehouse Market - Findhorn - Deli, Pizza & Bakery ///riverside.save.published
- Un Petit Cafe - Findhorn - Beachside coffee van ///converged.visitors.downfield

Restaurants
- Happy Haddock - Macduff - Local chip shop ///ticking.custodian.someone
- Bridgeview Restaurant - Banff - Lovely views of the sea
- Rockfish - Banff - Sit in & Takeaway ///servers.blueberry.hugs
- The New Denver - Cullen - Homely decor ///prowling.admit.kilts
- Portknockie Fish & Chip Shop - Town centre chippy ///doted.tailwind.rashers
- Bijou by the Sea - Buckie - Waterfront restaurant ///repelled.outwit.baker
- The Captain's Table - Findhorn - Pub with fresh seafood ///bend.steams.pheasants

Where to Stay
on the Moray Firth and Sunshine Coast

Hotels, B&Bs & Self-catering
- Seafront Cottages - Sandhaven - Quirky seafront pods ///absorbs.convey.textiles
- The Davron Hotel - Rosehearty - Seafront hotel ///rationed.yawned.since
- Down On The Farm - Fraserburgh - Countryside glamping ///mixes.panthers.acted
- AC/DC Glamping - New Aberdour - Unique pods ///retrieves.anchovies.grins
- The Seafield Arms Hotel - Cullen - Historical hotel ///changes.tickling.buggy
- Banff Springs Hotel - Luxury 4* hotel ///decorator.hers.dozed
- Speyside Self Catering - Fochabers - Overlooking Rover Spey ///stiff.fury.fidelity
- Lossiemouth House - An 18th Century B&B ///brotherly.braved.truffles
- The Findhorn Village Centre & Hostel - Affordable stay ///shunning.slumped.junction

Campsites
- Portsoy Links Caravan Park ///empire.splint.weeds
- Sandend Holidays ///busy.squirts.catapult
- Cullen Bay Holiday Park ///decorated.compiler.minerals
- Findochty Caravan Park ///ethic.arching.disarmed
- Strathlene Holiday Park ///never.challenge.smiling
- Burghead Holiday Park ///equal.spirits.daffodils
- Findhorn Bay Holiday Park & Camping ///exactly.enjoy.desktops

52 Findlater Castle

Roadtrip Essentials
on the Moray Firth and Sunshine Coast

Food Shops
- Premier - Sandhaven ///shackles.sloping.tiny
- Aldi - Macduff ///leotard.oxidation.nodded
- Scotmid Coop - Macduff ///shun.squad.applied
- Morrisons Daily - Banff ///goofy.spinning.squad
- Co-op Food - Portsoy ///trickles.tiles.grapevine
- Co-op Food - Cullen ///dips.radiates.twee
- Lidl - Buckie ///brings.critic.expert
- Co-op Food - Lossiemouth ///echo.streetcar.evolves
- Findhorn Village Store ///interest.requests.flocking

Electric Vehicle Charging Points
- Tesco Superstore, Fraserburgh ///ooze.smarting.gadgets
- Pennan Harbour ///bracing.values.reserving
- Banff Greenbank ///march.inhabited.distanced
- Cullen Square, Buckie ///access.firepower.toasted
- WDC Scottish Dolphin Centre ///reefs.easy.caring
- Elgin Railway Station ///regard.closes.dwell
- Court House Lane Car Park ///thatched.films.multiples

Fuel Stations
- Asda Petrol Station - Sandhaven ///kiosk.careless.artist
- Gleaner, Union Road - Macduff ///thinking.yoga.sandpaper
- Shell - Banff ///director.panel.boast
- Regency Oils Ltd - Buckie ///burst.tomato.buggy
- Harbour Service Station - Lossiemouth ///lifeguard.raves.ships
- Seapark Filling Station - Kinloss ///disclose.thunder.freezers

Campervan Facilities
- Waste Disposal, Fresh water - Rosehearty boatyard ///plotter.lift.direct
- Fresh water, Public Toilets - Shore Street, Portsoy ///drives.cemented.sugar
- Fresh water, Public Toilets - Port Long Road, Cullen ///continued.ventures.gums
- Waste Disposal, Fesh Water - Silver Sands Holiday Park ///cringe.competing.munched
- LPG and fuel station - Seapark Filling Station, Kinloss ///disclose.thunder.freezers
- Laundry, Fresh Water - Inverness Road, Nairn ///costumes.lump.passports

48 Gardenstown

SIGHTS

Castles & Historical Sights
- 72. Old Bridge of Livet
- 73. Ballindalloch Castle and Gardens
- 77. Old Craigellachie Bridge
- 79. Balvenie Castle
- 81. Auchindoun Castle
- 82. Leith Hall Garden & Estate
- 83. Huntly Castle
- 84. Fyvie Castle
- 85. Haddo House

Distilleries
- 74. Glenfarclas Distillery
- 78. Speyside Cooperage Visitor Centre
- 80. Glenfiddich Distillery

Mountains
- 75. Ben Rinnes

Waterfalls
- 76. Linn Falls

Dufftown & The Whisky Trail

Tucked between forested hills and winding rivers, Dufftown and the surrounding Whisky Trail region is where Scotland's spirit (both literally and figuratively) runs the deepest. This is Speyside, the beating heart of Scotch whisky production, where world-renowned distilleries, ancient castles, and lush countryside come together to create a journey that is as rich and smooth as the drams you'll find here.

Driving into Dufftown, the self-proclaimed "Whisky Capital of the World," you're immediately wrapped in the comforting scent of malted barley and oak casks. This small town is full of big characters, with names like Glenfiddich and Balvenie calling it home. Distilleries where you can walk among the stills, meet the makers, and taste whisky that has been produced in this quiet corner for centuries. Nearby, the Speyside Cooperage offers a glimpse into the centuries old craftsmanship that underpins every bottle, while the Old Craigellachie Bridge, with its elegant ironwork, stands as a reminder of the ingenuity that flows through this land.

However, it's not only the whisky that draws people here. Towering above the valley, Ben Rinnes offers those who enjoy a hike panoramic views of the distilleries below. Cascading waterfalls like Linn Falls are perfect picnic spots, and the surrounding estates, such as Ballindalloch, Leith Hall, and Fyvie Castle, all tell the story of Speyside's aristocratic past with their grand gardens and stately architecture. Huntly Castle and Auchindoun stand in more haunting silence, their stone ruins echoing tales of old clan rivalries.

In this part of the NE250, life feels slower. Maybe you're toasting the day with a dram of Glenfarclas, wandering the gardens of Haddo House, or tracing the lineage of lords and lairds through medieval strongholds, the Dufftown and Whisky Trail region will not disappoint. You are invited to savour every moment, just like a good single malt.

72. Old Bridge of Livet

The Old Bridge of Livet, also known as the Packhorse Bridge, is a historic structure near the small village of Glenlivet dating back to at least the 18th century. This high arched stone bridge once facilitated the transport of goods across the River Livet and though now it is partially collapsed it remains a landmark within the local area. There is a small car park off the B9008, just east of the B9136 junction and an information plaque provides historical context. The surrounding area is nice for a short walk or picnic.

-> On the B9008 in Glenlivet; approximately 300 meters east of its junction with the B9136, you'll find a small car park with signage directing you to the bridge. A short walk leads to this historic 18th-century packhorse bridge spanning the River Livet. Dog-friendly with accessible paths. ///resurgent.panthers.repayment

73. Ballindalloch Castle and Gardens

Ballindalloch Castle and Gardens is one of Scotland's finest and best preserved inhabited castles. This 16th-century baronial castle is often called the "Pearl of the North" and has been home to the Macpherson-Grant family for over 450 years. The beautifully furnished rooms are filled with family heirlooms, fine art, and fascinating artefacts. There is a woodland walk and gardens to explore outside. Entry tickets are available for the castle and grounds or grounds only and will differ in price. Open Sunday-Thursday.

-> Dogs are allowed in the grounds but not inside the castle. The site is wheelchair accessible, and Wi-Fi is available in the main visitor area. ///sample.manages.exonerate

74. Glenfarclas Distillery

Glenfarclas Distillery is a family owned distillery and has been in the family since 1836. They offer a variety of friendly tours around the distillery with a tasting session at the end. It is incredibly interesting learning about the history of each distillery and about the process of how the whisky is made in the Moray region, one of Scotland's most prolific whisky regions. They also have some very expensive and exclusive whiskies for sale here if you are feeling loose with the purse strings.

-> No dogs allowed inside. The visitor centre is accessible, and Wi-Fi is available. ///comical.deck.daunted

75. Ben Rinnes

Located just outside of the small town of Dufftown sits Ben Rinnes, the highest free standing mountain in Moray. It is a relatively easy climb compared to some of the other mountains across Scotland, reaching only 841 metres in altitude. There is one main path up the mountain, leaving from a small car park.

The total walk is 8km and the ascent is 548 metres so it will take roughly around 3 hours to walk, depending how long you spend at the top. The views from the top are beautiful and expand over the Cairngorm National Park and surrounding areas.

-> *Dogs are welcome, but the hike is challenging and not accessible for those with mobility impairment. Parking can be found just off the B9009, nearby the Beatshach Bothy - ///meals.opts.blank*

76. Linn Falls

Linn Falls is a spectacular waterfall located in Aberlour. It is only a short walk through the woods with a relatively low incline from the town of Aberlour. You may notice the sweet smell of whisky flowing out of the Aberlour distillery as you pass by.

The waterfall is beside a well maintained pathway so it is easy to find. It is also accessible when not too strong and is a great pool for a wild swim. You can park in the town centre or in the parking area directly off the A95 at the end of Dowans Road.

-> *Parking can be found in the town centre or in the parking area directly off the A95 at the end of Dowans Road. Dogs are welcome. The walking trail has uneven terrain, so accessibility is limited.*

77. Old Craigellachie Bridge

Old Craigellachie Bridge is an impressive cast iron arch bridge built by the famous Scottish civil engineer Thomas Telford, completed in 1814 it was once the oldest surviving iron bridge in Scotland. Spanning the River Spey near the village of Craigellachie, it's a grand structure with gothic style towers at either end. Today, it's a pedestrian only crossing, offering stunning views of the river and surrounding countryside. If you are here in autumn you can expect the trees along the Spey blaze with colour.

->*There is a small parking area off the A941 beside the bridge. Dog-friendly with accessible paths.*
///coupler.growth.refreshed

78. Speyside Cooperage Visitor Centre
The Speyside Cooperage Visitor Centre is located in Craigellachie and is the only working cooperage in the UK where you can observe the journey of a cask. It offers a unique insight into the traditional craft of coopering. Since being established in 1947 the cooperage produces and repairs nearly 150,000 oak casks annually for distilleries across Speyside and beyond and with the cooperage being surrounded by many renowned distilleries on the Malt Whisky Trail, it is a must visit if you enjoy whisky.

There is a viewing gallery that you can observe skilled coopers at work, participate in interactive exhibits, and learn about the lifecycle of a cask. Tickets can be booked online and tours run Monday-Friday to adults and children 8+. Adult £10, junior £6.

-> There is a large car park at the front of the visitor centre. ///submit.match.squirts

79. Balvenie Castle
Balvenie Castle is a historic ruin that was once home to the powerful Comyn and Douglas families and dates back to the 12th century. Mary, Queen of Scots, visited the castle in 1562 and the castle was then abandoned in the early 18th century. It is situated just north of Dufftown and is now managed by Historic Environment Scotland. Tickets are available to buy and explore the castle. It is cheaper to buy tickets online, adult £6 and child £3.50.

-> The castle is open to the public from April to September and offers parking facilities and public toilets. Dogs are allowed in outdoor areas on a lead. The historic site has uneven surfaces, making accessibility difficult. ///horn.prank.prospers

80. Glenfiddich Distillery
Glenfiddich Distillery is unique because it's one of the few single malt distilleries in Scotland that remains family owned, having been established by William Grant in 1887. It is located at the heart of Speyside in Dufftown and is is one of the world's best selling and most awarded single malt whiskies. What Glenfiddich are incredibly proud of is their dedication to tradition and craftsmanship as they still use their own onsite cooperage, source water from the same Robbie Dhu spring, and manage every part of the whisky making process themselves.

A variety of tours are offered on their website. If you require mobility assistance, please make this known when booking.

Glenfiddich, means "Valley of the Deer" in Gaelic.

-> TNo dogs allowed inside. The visitor centre is accessible, and Wi-Fi is available. ///cleanser.gravel.cave

79 Balvenie Castle

81. Auchindoun Castle

Auchindoun Castle is a fascinating 15th century ruin steeped in history perched on a hilltop near Dufftown. It is believed to have been constructed around 1479 by Thomas Cochrane, a favourite of King James III, the castle later came under the ownership of the Ogilvy family and subsequently the Gordons. During a feud in 1571, all of the occupants of Corgarff Castle were murdered by the Gordon's. The castle was eventually abandoned and fell into ruin by the 18th century.

Auchindoun Castle is managed today by Historic Environment Scotland and it is open all year round with no entry fee. Explore the thick stone walls and remnants of its defensive structures still standing. There are also fantastic views of the surrounding countryside.

-> *Access to the castle involves a short walk from a small car park located off a single-track road. Dog-friendly but requires a walk across rough terrain. Not accessible for wheelchairs. ///trickles.twins.prettiest*

82. Leith Hall Garden & Estate

Leith Hall, Garden & Estate features a 17th century house, on the site of the medieval Peill Castle, which served as the ancestral home of the Leith-Hay family for nearly three centuries. During World War I, the hall functioned as a temporary Red Cross hospital, treating over 500 patients and in 1945, the family donated the property to the National Trust for Scotland.

Enjoy the beautiful gardens and waymarked woodland trails to explore, an 18th-century stable block, and an ice house.

If you are an NTS member you will have free entry and parking. An adult ticket is £16 with concession and family options available. It is also possible to enter the castle for a guided tour if you book a visit online.

-> *Dogs are welcome in the gardens but not inside the hall. The site has accessible pathways and likely offers Wi-Fi in the visitor centre. ///grinning.applauded.smaller*

83. Huntly Castle

Huntly Castle, located in Aberdeenshire, is an impressive ruin that tells the story of Scotland's medieval and Renaissance past. Originally built as a motte-and-bailey fortress in the 12th century, it later became the grand seat of the powerful Gordon family. The castle is renowned for its elaborate stone carvings, including the intricate inscriptions and heraldic emblems that showcase the Gordons' wealth and influence.

Despite it now being in a ruined state, you can still admire and imagine the once luxurious great hall and rooms. Huntly Castle played a role in Scotland's turbulent past, including the Wars of Independence and the Jacobite uprisings. The castle is managed today by Historic Environment Scotland and tickets are available to buy and explore the castle. It is cheaper to buy tickets online, adult £7.50 and child £4.50.

-> *Managed by Historic Environment Scotland, dogs on leads are welcome in outdoor areas. Parking is available. ///handbags.trickling.quail*

84. Fyvie Castle

Fyvie Castle is a fine example of Scottish Baronial architecture, located in the heart of Aberdeenshire. The earliest information about Fyvie Castle dates back to the 13th century when it was the site of an open air court held by Robert the Bruce. The castle later became home to a series of noble families, each leaving their mark with grand expansions and extravagant interiors. A collection of ghost stories are also held in Fyvie Castle.

The castle grounds are extremely picturesque, with a beautiful loch and gardens that are very pleasant to walk around. Containing one of the largest bodies of water in the area as well as peaceful stretches of woodland, this is a great place to look out for wildlife such as red squirrels, foxes, swans, swifts and toads.

Fyvie Castle is part of the National Trust for Scotland therefore if you are a member, you will get entry into the castle and parking for free. An adult ticket is £17 with concession and family options available.

-> *Dogs on leads are permitted in the grounds but not inside the castle. The property provides accessible facilities, including parking and toilets. Wi-Fi is available in certain areas, such as the tearoom. ///sculpting.advantage.housework*

85. Haddo House

Haddo House is a grand 18th century stately home known for its elegant Georgian architecture with Victorian influences. Originally designed by William Adam in 1732, the house was lavishly remodeled in the 1880s, blending the refined elegance of Georgian architecture with the grandeur of a Victorian interior. Inside, generations of the Gordon family, who lived here for 400 years are commemorated through portraits, highlighting their significant role in Scottish history. More recently, during World War II, Haddo took on a new role as a maternity hospital, where over 1,200 babies were born.

Haddo House is surrounded by extensive gardens and flower beds and is now managed by the National Trust for Scotland. Use the postcode AB41 7LE , which will direct you via the only public access route from Raxton crossroads. Avoid relying on sat-navs, as they tend to suggest private roads. Pay & Display parking is available in the country park's large car park (not operated by the National Trust for Scotland), but NTS members visiting for a house tour receive free parking, you just need to request a validated ticket from the shop when booking. An adult ticket is £17 with concession and family options available and NTS members go free.

-> *Dogs on leads are welcome in the garden and grounds but not inside the house. The site offers accessible parking and pathways. Wi-Fi is available in the on-site café. ///rebounded.compress.freed*

Where to Eat
on the Dufftown & The Whisky Trail

Cafes
- **Fresh!** - Aberlour - Highstreet cafe serving fresh food ///sampled.triangle.spectacle
- **The Bank Cafe** - Huntly - Wide range of food options ///widget.dined.roadblock
- **The Gather'n Cafe** - Aberlour - Quirky cafe with a cosy interior ///stamp.dunk.ivory
- **The Coffee Pot** - Dufftown - Serving food and cakes ///worth.pretty.watchdogs
- **Cosy Coo Cafe** - Dufftown - Coffee & Gift shop with food ///posts.impresses.unto
- **Square Roots Cafe** - Keith - Cosy interior and delicious cakes ///scary.roving.helpfully
- **Traffords Coffee House** - Turriff - Serving fresh scones ///laminated.prelude.processor
- **Harry Gow Bakery** - Keith - Famous chain bakery ///lilac.jotting.cello

Restaurants
- **Dowans Hotel & Restaurant** - Aberlour - Victorian mansion ///practical.rainbow.securing
- **Highlander Inn** - Craigellachie - Huge whisky selection ///vibrate.manage.decorator
- **The Wee Puffin** - Grantown-on-Spey - Family-friendly restaurant ///chat.penned.joystick
- **Spice of India** - Dufftown - A local favourite Indian ///armful.months.goggles
- **Toots** - Aberlour - Inside the Station Hotel ///tracking.refuses.waltz
- **Tulchan Feast** - Grantown-on-Spey - BBQ restaurant ///sedative.flitting.prelude

Where to Stay
on the Dufftown & The Whisky Trail

Hotels, B&Bs & Self-catering
- The Mash Tun Hotel - Aberlour - Guesthouse with whisky bar ///nylon.from.ranch
- The Aberlour Hotel - Town centre & family-run ///cadet.beak.done
- Whisky Capital Inn - Dufftown - Huge collection of whiskies ///delusions.freezing.unfilled
- Alderwood B&B - Dufftown - Situated in the countryside ///lifted.dragonfly.hexes
- Gordon Arms Hotel - Huntly - Town centre hotel ///miracle.reverses.blaze
- Dunedin House - Huntly - Family-friendly and luxurious ///prawn.suits.twice

Campsites
- Speyside Gardens Caravan Park ///deprive.fussy.stay
- Dufftown Campsite ///jump.pyramid.clutches
- Huntly Castle Caravan Park ///sundial.snuggled.scowls
- Grantown on Spey Caravan Park ///papers.leaky.pine
- Grampian Campervan Aire & Campsite ///skate.stocked.demotion
- Speyside Camping and Caravanning Club Site ///frowns.restores.contexts

77 Old Craigellachie Bridge

Roadtrip Essentials
on the Dufftown & The Whisky Trail

Food Shops
- Co-op Food - Aberlour ///offer.supposing.cushy
- Mace - Aberlour ///ballparks.melt.attention
- Co-op Food - Dufftown ///pile.soonest.collides
- Londis - Craigellachie ///flank.blunders.screaming
- Tesco Superstore - Keith ///spike.burn.implanted
- Asda Supermarket - Huntly ///reds.marsh.loses
- Tesco Superstore - Huntly ///movies.aboard.fade

Electric Vehicle Charging Points
- Market Muir, Huntly ///testy.ombudsman.gently
- Dufftown Community Centre ///vast.scanner.pursue
- Speyside Gardens Caravan Park ///deprive.fussy.stay
- Linn Brae, Arberlour ///headline.nosedive.logo
- Craigellachie Filling Station ///passes.snippets.trudges

Fuel Stations
- Ashgrove Filling Station - Cairnie ///abandons.sparkle.gums
- Esso - Grantown-on-spey ///probable.averts.roadshow
- Tesco Petrol Station - Huntly ///reclaimed.skid.corded
- Gulf - Huntly ///storage.recap.riverside
- Gulf - Keith ///linen.classmate.caressed
- Tesco Petrol Station - Keith ///shuttled.cavalier.dock

Campervan Facilities
- Fresh Water, Public Toilets - Ashgrove Filling Station, Cairnie ///abandons.sparkle.gums
- Fresh Water, Pub Stopover (upon custom) - Fiddichside Inn ///locator.gobblers.kings
- Waste Disposal, Fresh Water, Overnight Aire ///skate.stocked.demotion
- Fresh Water, Overnight Aire - Glenlivet bike park ///brothers.stars.remaking
- Fresh Water - Londis Grantown-on-Spey ///trickster.last.keep

Glenfarclas Distillery

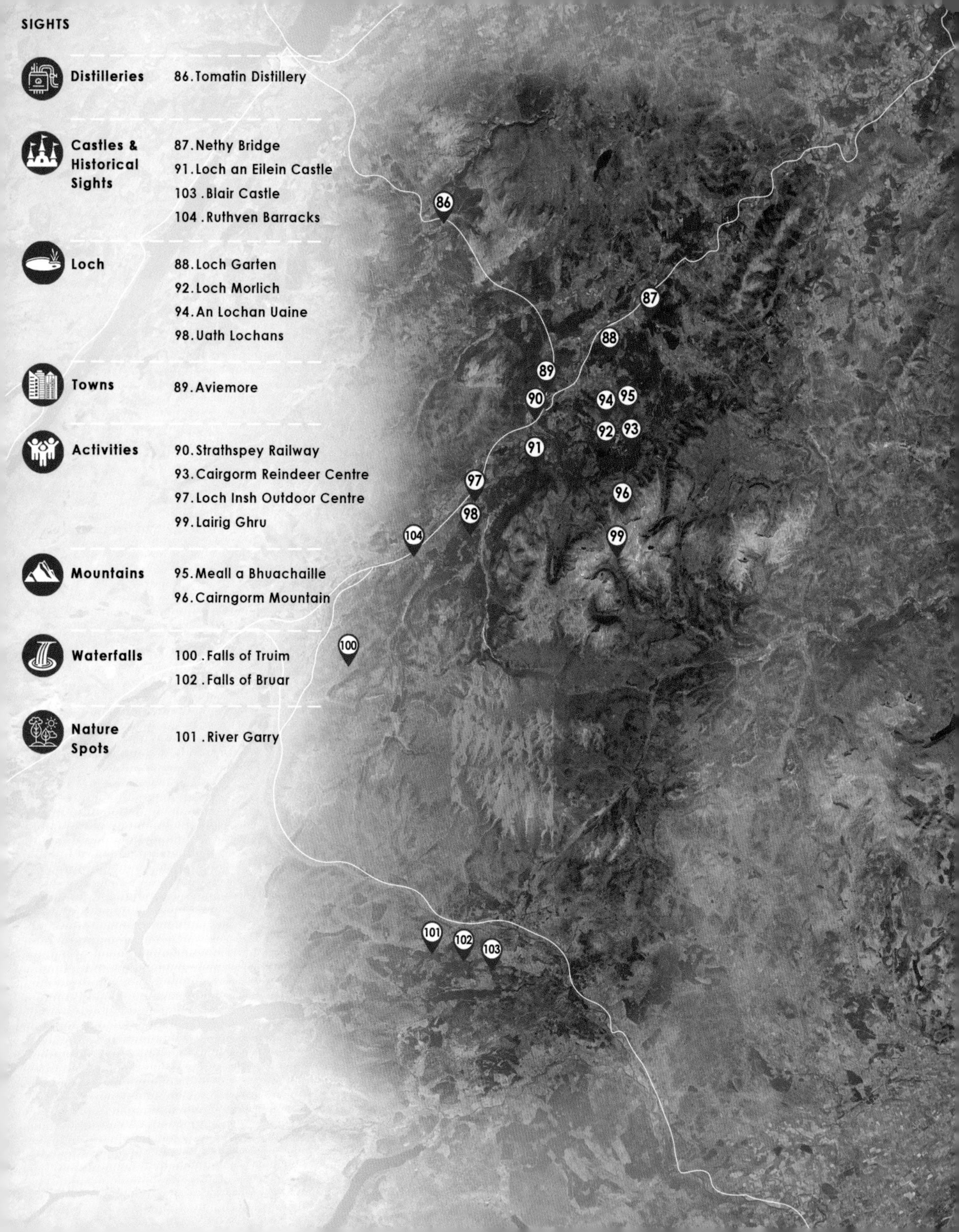

SIGHTS
Distilleries
86. Tomatin Distillery
Castles & Historical Sights
87. Nethy Bridge
91. Loch an Eilein Castle
103 . Blair Castle
104 . Ruthven Barracks
Loch
88. Loch Garten
92. Loch Morlich
94. An Lochan Uaine
98. Uath Lochans
Towns
89. Aviemore
Activities
90. Strathspey Railway
93. Cairgorm Reindeer Centre
97. Loch Insh Outdoor Centre
99. Lairig Ghru
Mountains
95. Meall a Bhuachaille
96. Cairngorm Mountain
Waterfalls
100 . Falls of Truim
102 . Falls of Bruar
Nature Spots
101 . River Garry
86
87
88
89
90
94
95
92
93
91
97
96
98
104
99
100
101
102
103

The Cairngorms

The Cairngorms hold a special place in our hearts. Long before we were road-tripping in campervans or writing guidebooks, we were children bundled into the back of our own family cars, wide-eyed with anticipation for our annual holidays to this magical corner of Scotland. Back then, days were spent building dams in icy rivers, playing hide and seek in the pine forests, and chasing deer tracks through the heather, and the love we felt for this wild place never left us. It's a love that deepened as we grew older and began to understand just how remarkable the Cairngorms truly are.

Although not on the official NE250 route, we felt that no trip to this beautiful part of Scotland would be complete without at least dipping your toes in this region. As the largest national park in the UK, the Cairngorms are a vast, untamed wilderness of ancient Caledonian forest, snow streaked mountains, glittering lochs, and thriving wildlife. This is a place where red squirrels dart through the treetops, golden eagles soar overhead, and herds of reindeer still roam freely on the Cairngorm plateau. Whether you're seeking adventure or stillness, the Cairngorms offer it all. Some of our favourites are summiting the rugged peaks like Meall a' Bhuachaille, wandering the shores of Loch Morlich or exploring the remnants of Ruthven Barracks.

Picturesque towns like Aviemore and Nethy Bridge provide a perfect base for your explorations, and historic attractions such as the Strathspey Railway and Blair Castle add a cultural richness to the wild surroundings. Outdoor lovers can try everything from kayaking at Loch Insh to hiking through the spectacular Lairig Ghru pass. Whisky lovers will also find their place here, with distilleries like Tomatin offering a warm Highland welcome and a dram or two to toast your adventures.

For us, the Cairngorms are more than just a stop on the map, they're home to some of our happiest memories and most special moments. Whether it's your first visit or your fiftieth, we hope this incredible region captures your heart just as it did ours.

86. Tomatin Distillery

Tomatin Distillery dates back to 1897, with whisky production on the site believed to have occurred since the 16th century. It was once the largest malt distillery in Scotland during the 1970s and since Tomatin has focused on producing high quality single malts, including its signature 12, 14, and 18 year-old, as well as the lightly peated Cù Bòcan. Guided tours of the distillery are available to book on their website where you can learn about the whisky making process, enjoy tastings, and visit the well stocked shop featuring exclusive bottlings and merchandise.

-> *Wheelchair accessible, offers free Wi-Fi in the gift shop, and is located off A9, about 16 miles south of Inverness.*
 ///units.grocers.sourcing

87. Nethy Bridge

Nethy Bridge is a charming village within the Cairngorms National Park that was originally named Abernethy before being renamed in the 1860s to avoid confusion with another station on the railway network. The village is renowned for its historic and iconic Telford bridge that was built in 1810 over the River Nethy. The bridge can be found in the centre of the village crossing the lower stretch of the River Nethy just a mile upstream from where it flows into the River Spey, one of Scotland's top salmon rivers.

The Abernethy Highland Games are held in the centre of Nethy Bridge every year on the second Saturday of August.

-> Nethy Bridge is dog-friendly with great walking trails and pet-welcoming cafés. It has accessible facilities, free Wi-Fi, and is easily reached by car or bus from Aviemore.   ///shut.rucksack.trail

88. Loch Garten

Loch Garten is a peaceful loch tucked away in the ancient Caledonian pine forest of Abernethy, within the Cairngorms National Park. After becoming extinct in the UK in the early 20th century, ospreys returned to Loch Garten in 1954, marking the beginning of a successful conservation story.

The RSPB Loch Garten Nature Centre that sits beside Loch Garten allows the chance to observe these incredible birds during the breeding season through live cameras and telescopes. In addition to ospreys, the area is home to red squirrels, crested tits, dragonflies, and a variety of other wildlife so it is a great place for a gentle walk along the trails through the forest.

-> *The surrounding trails are suitable for wheelchairs and prams. ///cork.beside.calm*

89. Aviemore

Aviemore is the perfect base for an adventure in the Scottish Highlands. Sitting in the heart of the Cairngorms National Park this lively town offers something for everyone, whether you're into outdoor activities or just want to soak up the stunning scenery of the nearby lochs and Cairngorm Mountain Range.

In winter, it's one of Scotland's go to spots for skiing and snowboarding on the Cairngorm Mountain. The rest of the year, there's hiking, biking, wild swimming, and watersports at nearby Loch Morlich. Aviemore itself has a great mix of cosy cafes, pubs, and outdoor shops, and there's even the Highland Wildlife Park and Aviemore Kart Raceway close by.

-> *The town centre has plenty of parking, with a large one beside the LIDL supermarket. Dog-friendly around the town and accessible for all. Plenty of cafes are available with Wifi connection for customers. ///verbs.collision.cried*

90. Strathspey Railway - (Aviemore Station)

The Strathspey Railway is a beautifully restored heritage railway that runs between Aviemore, Boat of Garten, and Broomhill in the heart of the Cairngorms National Park. Starting from Aviemore Station, you can take a nostalgic journey on a vintage steam train and enjoy a relaxed 1 hour 40 minutes through stunning Highland scenery. You can choose one of the many ticket options, some offering light lunch or afternoon tea and take comfort in the lovingly restored carriages as you set off on the adventure.

-> *Located at the southern end of the town, parking beside the train station is limited. Parking is available elsewhere around the town centre. Dogs are allowed on board, however, not in the 1st Class or dining cabins. Wheelchair accessible. ///bound.eliminate.unloading*

91. Loch an Eilein Castle

Translated to "Loch of the Island," in Gaelic this peaceful freshwater loch within the ancient Caledonian pine forest of Rothiemurchus, just a few miles south of Aviemore. In the middle sits a ruined 14th-century castle which was once a stronghold of the Clan Mackintosh and has a rich history of clan battles and Jacobite intrigue. In the 18th century, the loch's water level was raised to facilitate timber transport, submerging the original causeway that connected the castle to the shore.

The setting is pure Highland magic - calm waters and ancient pine trees. You can't visit the island itself as it is remote but walking the well maintained 5.3 km (3.3-mile) circular trail around the loch gives you stunning views of the castle from all angles. It's an ideal spot for a gentle walk, a picnic, or just to sit and soak up the peaceful atmosphere. There are opportunities to spot red squirrels, crested tits, and ospreys which nest around the loch.

-> There is a car parking charge at Loch an Eilein, £1.50 per person or £4.50 per car. The trails around the loch is a flat gravel path. Dog-friendly and accessible for most. ///straying.weekend.claim

92. Loch Morlich

This beautiful loch sits amongst the Glenmore Forest Park, near Aviemore and is overlooked by the Cairngorm mountain range. Renowned for being the highest beach in the UK and it is the only freshwater beach in Scotland to have a Rural Beach Award. There is plenty to do at Loch Morlich whether you are looking for somewhere to go for a leisurely stroll through the forest or if you are prepared to brave the water. Loch Morlich Watersports operates from the beach and has a variety of equipment available for rental including canoes and kayaks. Afterwards you can heat up in the Boathouse Cafe.

-> *Located about 6 miles west of Aviemore. There is paid parking all along the side of Loch Morlich and a visitor centre with toilets at the northeastern end. Car park - ///daylight.mondays.grove Visitor centre - ///gossiped.behaving.bind*

93. Cairngorm Reindeer Centre

The Cairngorm Reindeer tours are held in Glenmore, a short drive from Aviemore. Reindeer were re-introduced to the Cairngorm Mountains in 1952, where they were once native after a number of causes had reduced them to extinction in the UK. The Cairngorms is the only sub-arctic habitat in the UK which is why they were brought here to be where they can thrive. Today there are over 150 reindeer in the herd and they have 10,000 acres upon the mountainsides to graze upon.

There are two options to see the reindeer, in the paddocks at the centre or on the hills on a guided hill tour. The hill tour is a very unique experience as you get to learn about each of the reindeer and meet them on the hill.

-> dogs aren't allowed on hill trips or in the paddocks. The shop and exhibition areas are wheelchair accessible, but the hill walks are not, and there's no public Wi-Fi on site.   ///squares.relies.reclining

94. An Lochan Uaine

The An Lochan Uaine, also known as the Green Loch, is hidden in amongst the Caledonian pines on a trail that leads towards the Ryvoan Bothy, a short walk from the Glenmore Visitor Centre. Translated from Gaelic, An Lochan Uaine, means 'The Green Lochan' and is pronounced oo-an-yi. The deep turquoise colour of the water gives the Green Loch its name which most likely comes from the algae that is present in the water, as well as the reflection of the surrounding green pine trees.

According to local folklore, the loch is said to get its colour from the local fairies washing their clothes in it. It is said that when we are walking in this area we should wear something green to pay respect to the fairies. There are many great walking trails to enjoy in this area of the Cairngorms National Park.

-> A beautiful, dog-friendly woodland walk. Terrain is uneven, making accessibility limited. ///prosper.pouch.wimp

95. Meall a Bhuachaille

Hiking Meall a' Bhuachaille is one of the best ways to experience the Cairngorms without venturing too far off the beaten path. The name means "Hill of the Herdsman," and while it's not the tallest peak in the area, the views from the summit are absolutely stunning, allowing you to take in the Cairngorm scenery from a less intimidating mountain to most in that area. From the top you will get panoramas of Loch Morlich, the surrounding pine forests, and the wild Cairngorm mountains beyond.

This Corbett sits just short of a munro at a height of 810 metres and the looped trail is 8.7km, taking around 2-3 hours to complete.

The trail is well marked and manageable for most walkers with a bit of fitness. Along the way, you'll pass by the Ryvoan Bothy, a simple stone shelter not too far from the magical green waters of An Lochan Uaine (the Green Loch).

-> *Parking is available beside the Loch Morlich Visitor Centre. Dog-friendly but a strenuous hike. Not accessible for wheelchairs. No Wi-Fi. ///grief.parkland.clerk (parking)*

96. Cairngorm Mountain

One of the first activities Aviemore had to offer was access to the Cairngorm Mountains, the snowiest place in Scotland. During the winter months the Cairngorm Ski Resort becomes popular with skiers and snowboarders ready to test out the fresh snow on the slopes. Equipment is available to hire if you don't have your own. You may also want to try out the mountain tubing slides here, suitable for both adults and children. The Funicular Railway also takes you to the top of the slope, where on a sunny day the views are incredible! At the base station, you'll find the Cairngorm Café and shop, along with accessible toilets and paid parking.

-> Drive along the N59 road towards Achill Island, and follow the signs directing you to the viewpoint.
///placidly.shatters.pacers

97. Loch Insh Outdoor Centre

Loch Insh Outdoor Centre has been a hub for adventure since its establishment in 1969. Originally founded as the Cairngorm Canoeing and Sailing School, the centre has evolved into a comprehensive outdoor facility offering a variety of activities year round such as sailing, canoeing, and paddleboarding. Winter brings opportunities for skiing and snowboarding on the dry slope on site. The Boathouse Restaurant provides hearty meals made from locally sourced ingredients and has lovely views overlooking the loch.

As well as being a great place to get involved in outdoor activities, Loch Insh Outdoor Centre also has scenic accommodation options ranging from chalets to campervan pitches overlooking the loch.

-> Dogs are allowed in outdoor areas. The centre is accessible, and Wi-Fi is available. ///fixture.graphics.slanting

98. Uath Lochans

The Uath Lochans, pronounced "wah lochans" meaning the hawthorn small lochs are a hidden gem in the Cairngorms National Park. These four small lochans are surrounded by ancient Scots pine forest and overlooked by dramatic crags. It is an incredibly peaceful place to go for a walk, whether that be taking an easy trail around the lochans or a longer route up Farleitter Crag to get the beautiful view over the lochans and Glen Feshie and beyond. On a calm day, you'll spot dragonflies skimming the water which is why this place is often called the "Dragonfly Lochs." You may also hear the calls of ospreys overhead. It's quiet, unspoiled, and feels a world away from the busier parts of the Cairngorms.

-> Dog-friendly woodland walks. May be challenging for accessibility. No Wi-Fi. Parking - ///insolvent.passwords.alike

99. Larig Ghru

The Lairig Ghru is the most well known hill passes in Scotland, the path linking Aviemore and Braemar, met at the halfway point by the Corrour Bothy.

Walking from Aviemore to the Corrour Bothy is 43km that can be split over days. It takes around 7-8 hours to walk through this beautiful scenery over paths and some rough terrain. At the beginning, the walk is flat through forestry paths and it is well signposted to the Lairig Ghru. After around 10km, the forestry paths will disappear and you will be more open and walking in amongst the mountains. The views are absolutely incredible, especially on a clear day.

The Lairig Ghru reaches an altitude of 835m and at the highest point the path becomes lost underneath fallen boulders which is where the walk becomes incredibly tough. Along the walk, you will notice storm shelters made from rocks. This shows the extreme conditions that this landscape can experience.

Look out for the Cairns that people have built to show where the path leads if it has got lost due to boulders.

The Corrour Bothy is one of the most famous bothys in Scotland, therefore if you want to stay in the bothy, you will need to arrive early. It is worth bringing a tent with you as well in case there is no space. The bothy sits beneath the Devils Point on the banks of the River Dee which is the perfect way to cool off after a long hike if the weather is nice.

->The trail begins in either Aviemore or Braemar and leads up and over the Cairngorms. This should not be attempted without mountaineering experience and the correct equipment. Not accessible. Dog-friendly.

100. Falls of Truim

The Falls of Truim is a hidden gem just south of Newtonmore, tucked away beside the River Truim in the Cairngorms. These small but beautiful waterfalls are easy to reach, making them a perfect stop if you're exploring the area or driving along the A9. The falls cascade through rocky outcrops, surrounded by peaceful woodland and open moorland, offering a lovely spot for a short walk or picnic.

What makes the Falls of Truim special is the tranquillity, you'll often have the place to yourself, with only the sound of rushing water and birdsong for company. It's an ideal place to stretch your legs, take some photos, and enjoy a moment of calm away from the busier tourist spots or to break up your journey.

-> Dog-friendly woodland walks. May be challenging for accessibility. No Wi-Fi. Parking - ///unionists.dwell.irritate

101. River Garry

The River Garry winds its way through the heart of the Highlands, from Dalwhinnie down towards Blair Atholl, offering stunning scenery and plenty of opportunities to explore. One of the most stunning spots is the Pass of Killiecrankie, where the river surges through a steep, wooded gorge.

In autumn, the River Garry becomes a stage for one of nature's most impressive sights, leaping salmon. It is a great place to stop and watch as these powerful fish fight their way upstream to their spawning grounds, often seen at the Linn of Tummel or just below Killiecrankie. It's an incredible sight if you time it right!

-> Dog-friendly woodland walks. May be challenging for accessibility. No Wi-Fi. Parking -///noise.darkest.relieves

102. Falls of Bruar

The Falls of Bruar are a must visit if you're in the area or visiting the House of Bruar, also known as the "Harrods of the Highlands". The cascading waterfalls tumble dramatically through a deep gorge, surrounded by towering Scots pines and peaceful woodland. The poet Robert Burns visited in 1787 and was so taken by the scenery that he penned a poem urging the Duke of Atholl to plant trees here, and thankfully, the Duke listened! Today, the falls are framed by lush greenery, making the circular walking route a picturesque experience.

->Dogs are welcome, but the steep path may be difficult for those with mobility issues. Parking - ///refreshed.rainfall.showdown

103. Blair Castle

Blair Castle is a beautiful historic fortress that has served as the ancestral home of Clan Murray for over seven centuries. The castle's architecture reflects its rich history, transitioning from a medieval stronghold to a Victorian baronial mansion. Tickets are available to purchase to explore The 30+ rooms filled with artifacts, antiques, and art, as well as the newly introduced 'Below Stairs' exhibition, which offers an interactive look into the lives of the 19th century servants who worked at the castle. The surrounding 220 acre estate features the nine acre Hercules Garden, a restored Georgian walled garden, Diana's Grove with towering trees, and the ruins of St. Bride's Kirk, the burial site of Jacobite leader Bonnie Dundee. Tickets for the garden can be bought separately.

-> Dog-friendly in its gardens and grounds, though not inside the castle itself. It has good accessibility, free Wi-Fi in the main areas, and is easy to find just off the A9 near Blair Atholl. ///lively.screaming.theme

104. Ruthven Barracks

Ruthven Barracks, located near Kingussie in the Cairngorms National Park, is a historic military site built between 1719 and 1721 following the Jacobite rising of 1715. It was constructed atop a medieval castle mound and the barracks were designed to house government troops and enforce the Disarming Act of 1716. The complex comprises two large three storey blocks and enclosing walls with bastion towers, featuring loopholes for musket firing. In 1746 during the Jacobite rising, the barracks were destroyed by retreating Jacobite forces after the Battle of Culloden. Today, the ruins stand as a scheduled monument, offering visitors an insight into Scotland's wild history. The site is free to visit and open year round, providing panoramic views of the surrounding landscape.

-> Dog-friendly. A flat, gravel path leads up to the castle. Internal access my be difficult for those with mobility impairments
   Parking - ///bashful.latitudes.streak

92 Loch Morlich

Where to Eat
in the Cairngorms

Cafes
- **Cafe Bistro** - Kingussie - Wide range of food ///simulates.deck.boarding
- **Osprey Coffee House** - Boat of Garten - Local art for sale ///claps.searching.contracting
- **Route 7 Cafe** - Aviemore - Cycle themed ///unveils.backward.searching
- **The Barn at Rothiemurchus** - Aviemore - Locally sourced ///speakers.porridge.editor
- **Old Post office Cafe Gallery** - Kincraig - Beautiful art for sale ///ticked.indicated.bath
- **Laggan Stores Coffee Bothy & Gallery** - Wide range of goods ///mason.fastening.vouch
- **Blair Atholl Watermill** - Inside the old watermill ///prance.laying.clerk

Restaurants
- **Boathouse Restaurant Loch Insh** - Great outdoor activities ///trailer.unrated.condition
- **The Inverdruie Restaurant** - Inside the Coylumbriudge Hotel ///debating.purifier.ending
- **Aspects Restaurant** - Aviemore - Fine dining ///debating.purifier.ending
- **Letter Box Restaurant** - Newtonmore - Cosy cafe vibes ///rate.apprehend.curls
- **The Winking Owl** - Aviemore - Warm and weolcoming pub ///carry.scrubbing.absorb
- **The Old Bridge Inn** - Aviemore - Cosy pub with fireplace ///plodding.face.input
- **The Pine Marten Bar** - Dunbar - Popular with hikers ///isolated.jumbo.hunches
- **Ptarmigan Restaurant** - Located at the top of the mountain ///bumpy.tripling.typed

99 Lairig Ghru

Where to Stay
in the Cairngorms

Hotels, B&Bs & Self-catering
- Balavil Hotel - Newtonmore - Quaint highlands hotel ♿ 📶
- Richmond Arms Hotel - Tomintoul - Old world mansion house ♿ 📶 🐾
- Hotel Square - Tomintoul - Elegant building in heart of town ♿ 📶 🐾
- Broomfield Bothy - Drumuillie - Quirky lodge with sauna ♿ 📶 🐾
- Atholl Arms Hotel - 19th-century hotel near castle 📶 🐾
- Glenfeshie Hostel - Kingussie - Tranquil location ♿ 📶 🐾
- Rowan Tree Country Hotel - Built in an 18th-century coaching inn ♿ 📶 🐾

Campsites
- Cairngorm Motorhome Park ///baroness.agreement.fuss 🐾
- Invernahavon Caravan Park ///fearfully.convey.paths ♿ 📶 🐾
- The Bowling Club Camp Site ///ringside.pushing.arranged
- Loch Morlich Campsite ///lyricism.treatment.widely ♿ 📶 🐾
- Rothiuemurchus Campsite ///lunged.barstool.gearing ♿ 📶 🐾
- High Range Campsite ///handsets.headsets.barn ♿ 📶 🐾

96 Cairngorm Mountain

Roadtrip Essentials
in the Cairngorms

Food Shops
- **Co-op Food** - Grantown-on-Spey   ///firmly.clutches.springing
- **Fiona's Wholefoods & Refills** - Grantown-on-Spey   ///slides.tint.grub
- **Co-op Food** - Aviemore   ///bill.overlaid.many
- **ALDI** - Aviemore   ///tile.fermented.panicking
- **M&S Simply Food** - Aviemore   ///vessel.bill.ignites
- **Co-op Food** - Kingussie   ///tangible.bunny.hobbyists

Electric Vehicle Charging Points
- **Rie-Achan Road Car Park**   ///pinches.tiger.sharpens
- **Premier Inn Aviemore**   ///saddens.requiring.corn
- **Lecht Ski Centre**   ///alienated.showering.tubes
- **Ballater Golf Club**   ///initiated.removable.trickster
- **ChargePlace Scotland Charging Station**   ///bright.lion.momentous
- **The Seelies, Kingussie**   ///knocking.notch.belonged

Fuel Stations
- **Esso** - Grantown-on-Spey   ///probable.averts.roadshow
- **BP Services** - Aviemore   ///wishes.hesitate.kiosk
- **Esso** - Newtonmore   ///restrict.marker.stated
- **Dalwhinnie Service Station**   ///bundles.youths.testing

Campervan Facilities
- Waste Disposal, Puiblic Toilets - Grantown-on-Spey   ///palace.stiletto.bookshop
- Public Toilets, Nethy Bridge   ///shut.rucksack.trail
- Public Toilets & Showers - Grantown-on-Spey Leisure Centre   ///screen.probably.landed
- Waste Disposal, Fresh Water, Overnight Aire - Carrbridge   ///surprised.admit.enable
- Public Toilets & Showers - Aviemore   ///cabbies.captions.hothouse
- Waste Disposal, Fresh Water, Overnight Aire - Cairngorm Mountain   ///educates.markets.meals
- Public Toilets & Showers - Kingussie   ///scope.stood.shipyards
- Fresh Water, Public Toilets - Newtonmore   ///bordering.stun.trophy

15 Dunnottar Castle

Planning Your Route

Winding through some of Scotland's most dramatic and diverse landscapes, the North East 250 is a compact yet captivating road trip that offers a taste of everything this corner of the country has to offer including towering mountain passes, whisky-soaked glens, golden beaches, cute towns, and centuries of fascinating history. Designed as a circular route, it's the perfect way to explore the best of Aberdeenshire, the Moray Coast, and the eastern edge of the Cairngorms National Park.

We recommend beginning your journey in the charming village of Braemar, nestled deep in the Cairngorms, and travelling anti clockwise first east towards the North Sea, then tracing the shoreline past ancient castles and quaint fishing villages before looping inland through whisky country and back into the mountains. This route allows you to ease into the adventure with peaceful highland scenery before embracing the wild coastline and finishing with the rugged peaks and forests of the Cairngorms.

Whether you have just three days for a whistle stop tour of this part of Scotland or a leisurely week to fully immerse yourself in the region's hidden gems, there's a route to suit every schedule. In the following pages, we've outlined a series of carefully crafted itineraries to help you make the most of your NE250 adventure, whatever your timeframe, travel style or interests.

5-Day Itinerary on the North East 250

You don't need weeks on end to experience the magic of the North East 250. In just five days, this compact yet diverse road trip packs in ancient castles, dramatic coastlines, whisky distilleries, charming seaside villages, and the wild beauty of the Cairngorms. By looping from Braemar and travelling anti clockwise through Aberdeenshire's eastern edges, up to the Moray Firth, and back through whisky country, you can take in many of the NE250's most iconic highlights without rushing.

Day One - Braemar to Cruden Bay
Start your journey in **Braemar**, nestled in the heart of the Cairngorms. Stroll around the quaint village or visit nearby **Balmoral Castle** if it's open. Follow the A93 east through Royal Deeside, stopping at **Burn o' Vat** for a short walk into a hidden waterfall gorge. Continue towards the coast and arrive at **Cruden Bay**, where you can explore the eerie ruins of **Slains Castle** perched on the cliffs. Stay overnight in the village or nearby.

Day Two - Cruden Bay to Fraserburgh
Head north along the coast, stopping at **Newburgh Seal Beach** and the pretty harbour village of **Collieston**. Walk the dramatic clifftops at the **Bullers of Buchan**, and enjoy lunch with a sea view. In **Fraserburgh**, visit the **Kinnaird Head Lighthouse & Museum**, where maritime and castle history combine. Take a sunset stroll at the **Waters of Philorth Beach** before settling in for the night.

Day Three - Fraserburgh to Cullen
Travel the Moray Firth's "Sunshine Coast," dotted with fishing villages and castle ruins. Stop in **Pennan** and **Crovie** (tiny postcard-perfect villages tucked beneath towering cliffs). Walk the golden sands of **Cullen Bay** and catch golden hour at **Bow Fiddle Rock**, a natural sea arch jutting into the North Sea. Stay overnight in Cullen or nearby Portsoy.

Day Four – Cullen to Dufftown

Head inland into **Speyside**, the world-famous whisky region. Tour a distillery or two - **Glenfiddich**, **Glenfarclas**, and the **Speyside Cooperage** are top picks. Wander the ruins of **Balvenie Castle** and enjoy a peaceful forest walk to **Linn Falls**. Overnight in **Dufftown** or **Craigellachie**, surrounded by whisky heritage.

Day Five – Dufftown to the Cairngorms

Finish your loop by heading south through the **Cairngorms National Park**. Stop for a leg-stretch at **Loch Garten** or **Loch Morlich**, or visit the **Cairngorm Reindeer Centre** if time allows. If you're feeling active, take a short hike to **An Lochan Uaine**, the "Green Loch." Wind your way back to **Braemar**, completing your journey with views of rolling hills and high mountain passes.

54 Bow Fiddle Rock

10-Day Itinerary on the North East 250

For those with a little more time to spare, the NE250 rewards you with the chance to dive deeper into the heart of Scotland's northeast. This extended 10 day itinerary lets you explore the route at a relaxed pace, adding more castles, coastline, wildlife encounters, and Highland highlights without rushing through its rich tapestry of history, heritage, and natural beauty. Beginning in Braemar and looping anti clockwise through Royal Deeside, the Aberdeenshire coast, Moray, and the Cairngorms, this route is filled with unforgettable moments, from windswept cliff walks to whisky tasting in the Highland peaks.

Day One – Exploring Braemar
Start your journey in **Braemar**, a charming Highland village nestled in the Cairngorms. Take a gentle warm up walk to the atmospheric **Callater Stable Walkers' Bothy,** before returning north to explore the impressive **Braemar Castle**, with its star-shaped battlements and tales of Jacobite rebellion. Stay overnight in the area, soaking in mountain views and a sense of past grandeur.

Day Two – Royal Deeside
Head east into Royal Deeside, stopping at **Balmoral Castle**, the Queen's summer residence, and walk the trails to its hidden stone pyramids. Continue to the stark white tower of **Corgarff Castle**, an iconic sight along the route. Nearby, you can visit the historic **Lecht Mine** before continuing to **Tomnaverie Stone Circle**, an ancient ring with panoramic views. Stay overnight near Aboyne or Tarland.

Day Three – Waterfalls and Castles
Its a day full of ancient castles today! Begin with a forest walk to **Dess Waterfall**, then explore the fairytale pink tower of **Craigievar Castle.** You can choose to explore the inside of this castle or head on to the next sight. Explore **Castle Fraser** and its manicured estate before stopping at the immaculately preserved **Crathes Castle**, known for its painted ceilings and walled garden. Overnight in Banchory or continue towards Aberdeen.

Day Four – Aberdeen City Centre

Spend your day in and around Aberdeen. Explore the atmospheric ruins of **Dunnottar Castle**, perched above crashing waves, and pay a quick visit to the nearby town of Stonehaven. Head north to Aberdeen city and park up on the esplanade to enjoy a stroll along the colourful lanes of **Footdee**, a quirky old fishing quarter. You can then visit **Girdle Ness Lighthouse** on the waterfront before heading into the city centre for,
the **Union Terrace Gardens**, and **St Machar's Cathedral**, then explore the elegant architecture of **Marischal College**, the **William Wallace Statue**, and bustling **Union Street**. Stay the night in the city or along the seafront for a night with a view of the ocean.

25 St Machar's Cathedral

32 Newburgh Seal Beach

Day Five – East Coast Beaches

Leave the city behind and head north along the coast. Wander **Balmedie Beach**, stop by **Aikenshill Highlands** to spot Highland cows, and stretch your legs at **Newburgh Seal Beach**, where dozens of seals laze on the sandbanks. Continue to the dramatic ruins of **Slains Castle**, inspiration for the movie "Dracula", and gaze over the crashing waves at the **Bullers of Buchan**. Overnight in Cruden Bay or Peterhead.

Day Six – Peterhead & the Northeast

Visit **Peterhead Prison Museum** to dive into the darker side of Scottish history, then stop by **Rattray Head Lighthouse**, a remote spot often visited only by seabirds and seals. Walk the golden sands of **Waters of Philorth** and explore **Kinnaird Head Lighthouse and Museum**. As you follow the coast west, discover the tiny ruins of **Pitsligo Castle**, the **Pittulie Castle**, and end the day at peaceful **Rosehearty Beach**. Overnight nearby Peterhead or at the aire in Rosehearty.

Day Seven - Beaches on the North Coast
Start the day on the wide stretch of **Aberdour Beach**, then explore the postcard worthy village of **Pennan** tucked into cliffs, and take in the coastal views from **Cullykhan Beach** and the **Crovie Viewpoint**. Wind through to **Gardenstown**, a working fishing village stacked against the hillside. Visit the grand **Duff House** in Banff before staying overnight in **Portsoy** (grabbing a tasty ice cream) or nearby.

Day Eight – Cullen & Bow Fiddle Rock
Meander west to explore **Sandend**, then make your way to **Bow Fiddle Rock**, a stunning sea arch near Portknockie. Spend time wandering the sweeping sands of **Cullen Bay**, hunt for dolphins at **Strathlene**, and explore the curious double arched **Craigmin Bridge**. Stay near Fochabers or in a quiet countryside retreat near the Spey.

49 Duff House

Day Nine – Findhorn Bay

Head inland to explore the **WDC Scottish Dolphin Centre** at Spey Bay before moving on to **Elgin Cathedral** and the moody ruins of **Duffus Castle**. Visit **Pluscarden Abbey**, tucked deep in the forest, then stop at Benromach Distillery for a taste of Speyside's finest. Take a peaceful walk at **Findhorn Beach**, or explore **Roseisle Country Park**. Overnight at the Findhorn Park Up.

Day Ten – The Cairngorm National Park

Close your loop through the heart of the Highlands in our favourite place in Scotland. Visit the **Old Bridge of Livet** and **Ballindalloch Castle**, then sample whiskies at **Glenfarclas** or **Glenfiddich**. For epic views, hike **Ben Rinnes** or the stunning **Linn Falls**, then continue to **Aviemore** for forest walks, lochside adventures at **Loch an Eilein**, or a visit to the **Cairngorm Reindeer Centre**. Stay overnight surrounded by mountains at the Cairngorm Mountain range, toasting your final night on the NE250.

98 Uath Lochans

Two Weeks on the North East 250

The most relaxed and enjoyable length of time to spend exploring the NE250, 14 days allows you to slow down, rest, and truly absorb the magic of Scotland's northeast. With the additional time, you can enjoy more hikes, spend full afternoons in castles or museums, discover hidden coastal villages, and take time off from the road without missing out on any of the key sights.

Days 1-3: Royal Deeside & Highland Heritage

Start your journey in **Braemar**, a Highland village with regal roots and mountain charm. With three nights here, you can spend time exploring the local walking trails like the hike to **Callater Stable Bothy**, or even venture deeper into the hills for a taste of the **Lairig Ghru** to the west of Braemar. Take a full afternoon to explore **Braemar Castle**, then drive through the Dee Valley to visit **Balmoral Castle** and walk to its mysterious stone pyramids. With your third day, slow down at **Corgarff Castle**, visit the haunting **Lecht Mine**, or enjoy a picnic at **Tomnaverie Stone Circle**.

Days 4-5: Castles, Gardens & Aberdeen's Granite Heart

Spend a night inland to explore **Craigievar Castle**, **Castle Fraser**, and **Crathes Castle** at a relaxed pace, with time to stroll their sprawling gardens and estate woodlands. Continue to **Aberdeen** for two nights, giving you a full day to enjoy the city without rushing. Wander through **Duthie Park**, the **Kirk of St Nicholas**, and the **Union Terrace Gardens**, and soak up the city's cafe culture.

4 Balmoral Castle & Pyramids

54 Bow Fiddle Rock

Days 6-7: Coastal Views & Cute Villages

With two nights between **Cruden Bay** and **Peterhead**, you can enjoy both the dramatic sights and the slower rhythms of the coast. Walk the clifftop path to **Slains Castle**, peer into the sea caves of the **Bullers of Buchan**, and photograph the curious streets of **Footdee**. Spend time at **Newburgh Seal Beach**, watch the light change at **Rattray Head Lighthouse**, and explore **Peterhead Prison Museum** at your own pace.

Days 8-9: Hidden Castles & Moray Firth

Drive the coast westward, stopping at sleepy seaside villages like **Pennan**, **Crovie**, and **Gardenstown**. With two nights around **Banff** or **Portsoy**, take your time exploring **Duff House**, **Findlater Castle**, and the stunning **Bow Fiddle Rock**. The coast in this region is full of cliff walks that you can enjoy. To round off the day, visit Christie Alpacas and stay in the glamping pods for a stay that's both peaceful and delightfully fuzzy.

Days 10-11: Whisky Country

Base yourself in **Elgin** or **Forres** for two nights to enjoy the heart of Speyside without the rush. Visit **Elgin Cathedral**, **Duffus Castle**, and **Pluscarden Abbey**, and take a slow drive along the whisky trail, stopping at **Benromach**, **Glen Moray**, or **Glenfiddich** distilleries. For nature lovers, the forest walks at **Roseisle Country Park** and **Findhorn Bay** are ideal spots to unwind.

Days 12-14: Cairngorms & a Highland Farewell

End your journey with three nights in or around **Aviemore**. This gives you the freedom to explore the **Cairngorms** properly - whether hiking to **Loch an Eilein**, watching reindeer at the **Cairngorm Reindeer Centre**, or taking a trip on the **Strathspey Railway**. For the adventurous, climb **Meall a' Bhuachaille** or paddleboard on **Loch Morlich**. Don't miss a visit to **Ballindalloch Castle**, the **Speyside Cooperage**, and **Old Craigellachie Bridge** along the way.

63 Covesea Lighthouse

Index

Sights

Aberdeen Beach	91
Aberdour Beach	126
An Lochan Uaine	175
Auchindoun Castle	158
Aviemore	171
Ballindalloch Castle	152
Balmedie Beach	107
Balmoral Castle & Pyramids	71
Balvenie Castle	156
Belmont Street	94
Ben Rinnes	154
Benromach Distillery	141
Blair Castle	182
Bow Fiddle Rock	133
Braemar	69
Braemar Castle	70
Brodie Castle and Estate	141
Bullers of Buchan	112
Cairgorm Reindeer Centre	174
Cairngorm Mountain	178
Callater Stable Walkers' Bothy	69
Castle Fraser	75
Collieston	109
Corgarff Castle	72
Covesea Lighthouse	138
Craigievar Castle	74
Craigmin Bridge	135
Crathes Castle	78
Crovie Village Viewpoint	126
Cruden Bay	110
Cullen Bay	131
Cullykhan Beach	126
Dess Waterfall	74
Drum Castle	78
Duff House	128
Duffus Castle	139
Dunnottar Castle	80
Duthie Park	92
Elgin Cathedral	136
Falls of Bruar	182
Falls of Truim	181
Findhorn Bay Nature Reserve	140
Findhorn Beach	140
Findlater Castle	130
Footdee	90
Fyvie Castle	159
Gardenstown	128
Girdle Ness Lighthouse	90
Glen Moray Distillery	137
Glenfarclas Distillery	152
Glenfiddich Distillery	156
Gordon Castle	135
Greyfriars Church	96
Haddo House	160
Huntly Castle	159
Kildrummy Castle	74
Kinnaird Head Lighthouse	123
Kirk of St Nicholas	94
Lairig Ghru	180
Lecht Mine	72
Leith Hall Garden & Estate	158
Linn Falls	154
Loch an Eilein Castle	172
Loch Garten	171
Loch Insh Outdoor Centre	178
Loch Morlich	173
Lossiemouth	137
Marischal College	97
Meall a Bhuachaille	177
Muir of Dinnet NNR	72
Nelson's Tower	141
Nethy Bridge	170
Newburgh Seal Beach	108
Old Bridge of Livet	151
Old Craigellachie Bridge	155
Pennan	126
Peterhead Prison	112
Pitsligo Castle	125
Pittulie Castle	123
Pluscarden Abbey	139
Portsoy	129
Powis Gates	92
Rattray Head Lighthouse	113
River Garry	181
Rosehearty Beach	125
Roseisle Country Park	140
Ruthven Barracks	183
Sandend	129
Seaton Park	97
Slains Castle	110
Speyside Cooperage	156
Spynie Palace	137
St Andrew's Cathedral	97
St Machar's Cathedral	96
Strathlene	133
Strathspey Railway	171
Tomatin Distillery	169
Tomnaverie Stone Circle	73
Uath Lochans	179
Union Street	95
Union Terrace Garden	93
Waters of Philorth Beach	123
WDC Dolphin Centre	135
William Wallace Statue	97

Accommodation

Aberdeen Arms Hotel	82
AC/DC Glamping	144
Aikenshill House B&B	116
Alderwood B&B	162
Ardoe House Hotel & Spa	100
Atholl Arms Hotel	186
Balavil Hotel	186
Banff Springs Hotel	144
Broomfield Bothy	186
Buchan Braes Hotel	116
Cambus o'May Hotel	82
Cranford Guest House	82
Crathie Opportunity Holidays	82
Down On The Farm	144
Dunedin House	162
Glenfeshie Hostel	186
Gordon Arms Hotel	162
Haughton Arms Hotel	82
Hotel Square	186
Leonardo Hotel	100
Lossiemouth House	144
Malmaison Hotel	100
Palm Court Hotel	100
Richmond Arms Hotel	186
Rowan Tree Country Hotel	186
Seafront Cottages	144
Seaview Hotel	116
Speyside Self Catering	144
St. Olaf Golf Hotel	116
Tahuna Bothies	116
The Aberlour Hotel	162
The Brig Inn Hotel	100
The Davron Hotel	144
The Findhorn Village Hostel	144
The Green Inn Rooms	82
The Mash Tun Hotel	162
The Seafield Arms Hotel	144
The Ship Inn	82
Village Hotel - Aberdeen	100
Waverley Hotel	116
Whisky Capital Inn	162
Wildflower Eco Lodges	116

Campsites

Aden Caravan & Camping	116
Ballater Caravan Park	82
Braemar Caravan & Pods	82
Burghead Holiday Park	144
Cairngorm Motorhome Park	186
Craighead Holiday Park	116
Cullen Bay Holiday Park	144

Deeside Holiday Park	100
Dufftown Campsite	162
Feughside Caravan Park	82
Findhorn Bay Holiday Park	144
Findochty Caravan Park	144
Grampian Campervan Aire	162
Grantown on Spey	162
High Range Campsite	186
Hillhead Caravan Park	100
Huntly Castle Caravan Park	162
Invernahavon Caravan Park	186
Loch Morlich Campsite	186
Peterhead Marina Bay	116
Portsoy Links Caravan Park	144
Rothiuemurchus Campsite	186
Sandend Holidays	144
Seaview Caravan Park	100, 116
Seaview Caravan Park	116
Silverbank C&M Club Site	82
Speyside C&C Club Site	162
Speyside Gardens	162
Stonehaven C&M Club Site	82
Strathlene Holiday Park	144
Tarland C&C Club Site	82
Templars' Park	100
The Bowling Club Camp Site	186

Dining

210 Bistro	99
Amarone	99
Aperitivo Italian Restaurant	99
Aspects Restaurant	185
Bijou by the Sea	143
Birdhouse Cafe	81
Blair Atholl Watermill	185
Boathouse Loch Insh	185
Books and Beans	99
Borsalino	81
BrewDog DogTap	115
Bridgeview Restaurant	143
Cafe Andaluz	99
Cafe Bistro	185
Cafe Nineteen	115
Café Noir Coffee House	81, 99
Cherry Tree Cafe & Bistro	143
Clachan Grill	81
Clerkhill Fishbar	115
Coastal Cuppie	143
Coffee At The Kins	143
Cornkist	115
Cosy Coo Cafe	161
Dolphin Cafe	115
Dowans Hotel & Restaurant	161
Eli's Crafts, Cakes & Coffee	143
Farquharsons Bar & Kitchen	81
Fresh!	161
Gulay's Patisserie	143
Happy Haddock	143
Harbour Dunes	115
Harry Gow Bakery	161
Highlander Inn	161
Highlanders Bakehouse	81
Home Bakery	143
Kildrummy Inn	81
Kilmarnock Arms Hotel	115
Laggan Stores Coffee Bothy	185
Letter Box Restaurant	185
Maggie's Grill	99
Morad's Beach Front Café	99
Nikimax Cafe	115
No.10 Bar and Restaurant	99
Old Post office Cafe Gallery	185
Osprey Coffee House	185
Portknockie Fish & Chip Shop	143
Potarch Café	81
Ptarmigan Restaurant	185
Ride Coffee House	81
Rockfish	143
Rockpool Cafe	143
Route 7 Cafe	185
Scolty Cafe	81
Spice of India	161
Square Roots Cafe	161
SYMPOSIUM coffee house	115
Tarlair Cafe	143
Tarmachan Cafe	81
The Alford Bistro	81
The Bakehouse Market	143
The Bank Cafe	161
The Barn at Rothiemurchus	185
The Bothy	81
The Captain's Table	143
The Chinwag Cafe	115
The Coffee Apothecary	115
The Coffee Pot	161
The Cult Of Coffee	99
The Dunes Restaurant & Bar	115
The Gather'n Café	161
The Inverdruie Restaurant	185
The Long Dog Café	99
The New Denver	143
The Old Bridge Inn	185
The Pine Marten Bar	185
The Village Chipper	115
The Wee Puffin	161
The Winking Owl	185
Toots	161
Traffords Coffee House	161
Trellis Coffee Shop	115
Tulchan Feast	161
Un Petit Café	143
Wild Boar	99

Written:
Gemma Kerr
Campbell Kerr
Natasha Gooch

Photos:
Gemma Kerr
Campbell Kerr

Editing:
Campbell Kerr

Design:
Campbell Kerr
Shiva Shahriari (iOb Design)

Photo copyrights:
Copyright © 2025 Campbell Kerr, Gemma Kerr. All rights reserved. The moral rights of the authors have been asserted. All photos © 2025 Gemma Kerr and Campbell Kerr.

Author Acknowledgements:
Throughout the production of the book itself, as well as the years leading up to its conception, the support of the families and friends of both Gemma and Campbell have been unbelievable. Campbell would like to thank his family for the unquestioning support they have shown not only in this project, but in all of the crazy ideas and passions that he has shown throughout his life. Gemma would like to thank her family and close friends for the continuous support they have shown throughout this project and her many other adventures over the years.

Health, Safety, and Responsibility:
As with any outdoor and adventure activity, from land to water-based, there is always a level of risk with those discussed in this book. The locations in this book are all prone to dangerous conditions caused by nature, floods, droughts, high winds, severe rain, snow, and foggy conditions. While the authors of this book have gone to great lengths to ensure the accuracy of the information provided in this book, they will not be held legally or financially responsible for any accident, injury, loss or inconvenience sustained as a result of the information or advice contained in this guide. All activities that are discussed in this book are done entirely at the reader's own risk.

Scan the barcode below for access to the Destination NE250 map, showing all sights listed in this book

LIKE ANY PICTURES? GET A CANVAS PRINT
All pictures shown in this guide, as well as many others that were captured along the route, are all available for canvas print for you to enjoy in your home. Visit our website shown below for the full range of prints, or get in touch at the email below for any special requests.

Get in touch - contact@destinationearthguides.com

www.destinationearthguides.com